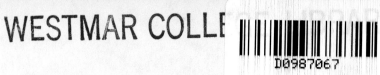

POLITICS AND ADMINISTRATION

POLITICS

AND ADMINISTRATION

A Study in Government

BY

FRANK J. GOODNOW, A.M., LL.D.

PROFESSOR OF ADMINISTRATIVE LAW IN COLUMBIA UNIVERSITY

NEW YORK / RUSSELL & RUSSELL

FIRST PUBLISHED IN 1900
REISSUED, 1967, BY RUSSELL & RUSSELL
A DIVISION OF ATHENEUM HOUSE, INC.
L. C. CATALOG CARD NO: 66-24696

PRINTED IN THE UNITED STATES OF AMERICA

PREFACE

THE purpose of this little work is to show, particularly from a consideration of political conditions as they now exist in the United States, that the formal governmental system as set forth in the law is not always the same as the actual system. The attempt is also made to indicate what changes in the formal system of the United States must be made, in order to make the actual system conform, more closely than it does at present, to the political ideas upon which the formal system is based.

This attempt has involved an analysis of the operations of government and a consideration of their interrelations, together with a study of the position of the political party and of its leaders, whom we are beginning to call " bosses."

The concrete remedies proposed are first, a greater centralization of our state administrative system, following the model of the national administrative system, in the hope of taking from the vast mass of administrative authorities the power which they now have of obstructing the execution of state laws, and of thus making it possible to relieve such administrative authorities from political tests for holding office; and, second, the subjection of the political party, as a political organ recognized by law, to an effective public control, in the hope of making the party and its leaders more responsive to the public will.

The author desires to acknowledge his indebtedness for valuable suggestions to his friend and colleague, Professor Franklin H. Giddings, who, at his request, kindly consented to read his manuscript.

FRANK J. GOODNOW.

COLUMBIA UNIVERSITY,
April 1, 1900.

TABLE OF CONTENTS

CHAPTER I

CHAPTER II

CHAPTER III

CHAPTER IV

CHAPTER V

CHAPTER VI

THE INFLUENCE OF THE GOVERNMENTAL, AND PAR-
    TICULARLY OF THE ADMINISTRATIVE, SYSTEM ON
    THE POSITION OF THE POLITICAL PARTY . . 133

CHAPTER VII

CHAPTER VIII

CHAPTER IX

CHAPTER X

POLITICS AND ADMINISTRATION

CHAPTER I

THE PRIMARY FUNCTIONS OF THE STATE

THE tendency of most writers on governmental subjects has been to confine their study to the more striking facts which become apparent as a result of considering alone the formal governmental organization. Thus, most writers on American government begin and end their work with the Constitution. Some, it is true, endeavor to treat of the history of the Constitution as well as its present form, but few have attempted to get back of the formal governmental organization and examine the real political life of the people. The cause of this method of treating our political institutions is unquestionably to be found in the fact that most of the writers who have left their impress on American political science have been lawyers, and are therefore not accustomed to look beyond the provisions of positive law.

No method of treatment, however, is more likely

to mislead the student in the formation of his judgment of a nation's real political life; for the character of a governmental system is determined just as much by extra-legal as by legal institutions. Indeed, it is not infrequently the case that extra-legal institutions have more influence in giving its character to a political system than the mere legal form in which it may be framed. Thus, Rome became an empire, preserving for a long time the outward forms of a republic. Thus, again, the public law of England makes provision for a Crown, a Privy Council, and a Parliament. But every one who knows anything about the English government knows that none of these institutions is to the real political life of the English people what the Cabinet is, — a body absolutely unknown to the English law.

Burgess, in commenting upon the distinction of sovereignty from government, which he has done so much to make clear, says: The "change from the old form to the new one, when it works itself out gradually and impliedly, so to speak, does not mark off the boundary sharply and exactly between the old and the new systems. Naturally the old state [sovereign] does not perceive the change at all, or at least not for a long time and not until after suffering many bitter experiences. It still expresses itself in the language of sovereignty.

It still struts about in the purple, unconscious that the garment is now borrowed. On the other hand, the new sovereignty comes very slowly to its organization." [1] What is here so forcibly said about sovereignty may be said with even greater truth about government, and particularly about a government which is based on a written constitution. No sooner is such an instrument adopted than political forces begin at once to interpret it and amend it until the actual political system becomes, almost without the knowledge of the people, quite different from the system as outlined in the constitution itself. In course of time, the changes actually made in the system will without doubt come to the knowledge of the people, and, it may be, will be incorporated in the formal constitution. But the actual system of government may be changed long before the formal government is changed.

No better example of this fact can be found than the method of electing the President of the United States. Although as provided by the Constitution, the President is formally elected indirectly by the people of the states, that is, by presidential electors who are elected by the people, hardly any one who votes for a presidential elector

[1] Burgess, *Political Science and Comparative Constitutional Law*, Vol. I., p. 69.

gives a thought as to his character. Every one is thinking of the presidential candidates put in nomination by the political parties. The party system has thus come to supplement — we may say indeed to amend — the Constitution, and no discussion of the constitutional method of electing the President would give a fair idea of the actual method of his election, which did not treat of the attitude of the political parties toward this matter.

Where the governmental system is not based on a written constitution, it is more probable that extra-legal institutions will be given a place in any theoretical discussion of the governmental system. For the constitution itself in such a country is largely a matter of custom. Custom must therefore be examined in order to set forth the constitution. It is not possible for the investigator altogether to omit the consideration of extra-legal institutions. For outside of them he may not have anything upon which to base his conclusions. It is for this reason that the modern treatment of the English governmental system is perhaps more satisfactory than that of the governmental system of the United States. By this is meant that a more exact and accurate account is ordinarily given of the operation and working of political forces. It is significant that the best description of the actual political system obtaining in the United States is given us by an Englishman, Mr. Bryce, who, accustomed in his own country to look behind the positive law to find its political system, and applying the methods to which he is accustomed to our system, has given us an admirable description of American political institutions.

Not only does the student of governmental subjects ordinarily fail to lay due stress on extra-legal institutions. He also is too apt to confine himself to constitutional questions, perhaps not considering at all the administrative system. The administrative system has, however, as great influence in giving its tone to the general governmental system as has the form of government set forth in the constitution.

Gneist was almost the first student of note to call attention to the importance of administrative institutions. He became convinced that the parliamentary system of government, originating in England and thence transplanted to the Continent, was not accomplishing there what it had accomplished in England. He therefore set to work to make a thorough study of English institutions, not merely what is known as the English Constitution, but the entire English system of government and particularly its administrative system. He arose from his study with the belief that English parliamentary government could not be understood apart from the English administrative system, and that the reason for the comparative failure of parliamentary government on the Continent was that an English superstructure had been raised on a Continental foundation. Such was the case, in Gneist's opinion, because the English system had been explained to Continental Europe by French writers like Montesquieu, De Lolme, and Benjamin Constant, who were acquainted merely with the relations of the English Crown to the English Parliament, and knew nothing of the English administrative system on which the English parliamentary system was based.[1] The rest of Gneist's life was successfully devoted to advocating such changes in the German administrative system as would make a proper foundation on which a system of parliamentary government similar to that developed in England might be built up.

If it be borne in mind that the political institutions of a people are to be found without, as well as within, the law, and that the constitution cannot be understood without a knowledge of the administrative system, it is believed that the political institutions of different peoples will show a much greater similarity than would be thought to exist were the consideration confined to the formal provisions of the constitutional law.

[1] Cf. Gneist, *English Constitutional History*, Preface.

The political life of man is largely conditioned by the fact of his humanity, the fact that he is man. Of course his degree of intelligence, his ideas of right and wrong, at different periods of his development, are by no means the same, and the form of government adopted at one stage of his development may have an important effect upon his later condition. But it is believed that the real political institutions of different peoples at the same stage of intelligence and morality will show a great similarity, even where the external forms of government appear very different. This similarity is due, as has been said, to the fact that after all man is man everywhere and at all times, and that all political organizations of men must therefore have ultimately the same ends, and must adopt in a general way the same methods for their satisfaction. Sometimes it may be that these political organizations will be adequately reflected in the formal governmental organization. At other times, and indeed most frequently, they will not be. The whole political life must be considered.

It is because of this similarity of the real political systems of different states that it is possible to conceive of the state as an abstraction. Just as we would be unable to conceive of a horse in the abstract, if concrete horses did not resemble each other, so would we be unable to think of the state

apart from the concrete examples of the states we
know, were there not great similarity between these
concrete states. This abstract conception of the
state is not only possible, but as a matter of fact
would seem to have been grasped by almost all writers on theoretical political science. This conception
is further the conception of a thing endowed with
life and capable of action. The state abstractly
considered is usually likened to an organism. This
analogy between the state and an organism has
been seen by many writers on politics. Hobbes, in
his *Leviathan*, would seem to have foreshadowed
the idea which has of recent years been so commonly accepted. Some writers even go so far as
to claim not so much that there is an analogy
between the state and an organism, but that the
state is actually an organism.[1] Others, however,
while believing that the biological analogy is a
dangerous one to emphasize, still speak of a social
mind and a social will, as if the action of political
organizations were the result of the exercise of a
real will by a person capable of willing. Thus
Giddings says:[2] "The primary result of association is an evolution of the individual mind. The
secondary result is an evolution of the social mind."
Again he says,[3] "Sociology is the science of men-

---

[1] See Posada, *Tratado de Derecho Administrativo.*
[2] *Principles of Sociology*, p. 132.   [3] *Ibid.*, p. 26.

tal phenomena in their higher complications and reactions, and of the constructive evolution of the social medium through which the adaptations of life and its environment become reciprocal."

Whatever may be the truth or error in this conception of the state, it is still true that political functions group themselves naturally under two heads, which are equally applicable to the mental operations and the actions of self-conscious personalities. That is, the action of the state as a political entity consists either in operations necessary to the expression of its will, or in operations necessary to the execution of that will. The will of the state or sovereign must be made up and formulated before political action can be had. The will of the state or sovereign must be executed, after it has been formulated, if that will is to result in governmental action. All the actions of the state or its organs, further, are undertaken with the object, either of facilitating the expression of this will or of aiding in its execution. This would seem to be the case whatever may be the formal character of the governmental system.

In a purely monarchic system the operations necessary to the expression of the state will are naturally much less complex than in a popular or democratic government. But they are in both cases of essentially the same nature. The same is true to an even greater degree of the execution of the state will. The form of government has little influence upon these conditions with the single exception that the less popular the government, the less is the function of executing the will of the state differentiated from the function of expressing that will. For the tendency of all monarchic governments is to concentrate governmental powers in the hands of the same authority. At the same time, the necessity for the division of labor makes it necessary, even in monarchic governments, to distinguish between these two functions.

The distinction between these two functions, further, is made necessary by psychological causes. In the case of a single person, who naturally both formulates and executes his will himself, it is necessary that this will be formulated before it is executed. In the case of political action it is necessary not only that the will of the sovereign be formulated or expressed before it can be executed, but also that the execution of that will be intrusted in a large measure to a different organ from that which expresses it. The great complexity of political conditions makes it practically impossible for the same governmental organ to be intrusted in equal degree with the discharge of both functions.

The fact is, therefore, that not merely may these two functions be distinguished in all kinds of governments, but that in every government more or less differentiated organs are established. Each of these organs, while not perhaps confined exclusively to the discharge of one of these functions, is still characterized by the fact that its action consists largely or mainly in the discharge of one or the other.   This is the solution of the problem of government which the human race has generally adopted.   It is a solution, further, which is inevitable both because of psychological necessity and for reasons of economic expediency.

It is upon this fundamental distinction of governmental functions that Montesquieu's famous theory of the separation of powers is based. In his *Esprit des Lois* (Book XI., Chap. VI.) he distinguished three powers of government which he called respectively the legislative, executive, and judicial.   This differentiation of three rather than two governmental functions was probably due to the fact that Montesquieu's theory was derived very largely from a study of English institutions. England was almost the only country of the civilized world which, at the time he wrote, made a clear distinction in its governmental organization between the executive and judicial authorities. This was made, it will be remembered, by the Act of Settlement passed in 1701, which prevented the Crown from removing the judges without the concurrent action of Parliament. It was only natural that Montesquieu should find, in the independence of the judiciary, the recognition of a judicial power separate from and independent of the executive power.

If, however, Montesquieu had carried his researches further, he would have seen that the existence of this third function of government, *i.e.* the judicial function, could not be predicated from the mere fact of the independence of the judges. A study of the powers of the judges of the higher courts, and particularly of the powers of the justices of the peace, would have shown conclusively that English political ideas were not reconcilable with the existence of three powers of government. Parliament, it is true, made the law, but so did the courts in their power of deciding concrete cases. The laws also were enforced by authorities which at the same time administered justice.

Montesquieu's theory of the existence of three powers of government is not, finally, accepted by the modern political philosophy of his own country. As one of the great writers on French administrative law, M. Ducrocq, says : "The mind can conceive of but two powers : that which makes the law, and that which executes it. There is no place therefore for a third power by the side of the first two."[1]

Montesquieu's theory involved, however, not merely the recognition of separate powers of functions of government, but also the existence of separate governmental authorities, to each of which one of the powers of government was to be intrusted. This part of his theory has had an enormous influence on the governmental organizations which have been established since Montesquieu wrote his *Esprit des Lois*.

This theory was, as to this point, carried much further than its author would have considered proper, and in its extreme form has been proven to be incapable of application to any concrete political organization. American experience is conclusive on this point.[2]

At the time our early constitutions, including the national Constitution, were framed, this principle of the separation of powers with its corollary, the separation of authorities, was universally accepted in this country. It was therefore with its corollary

[1] Montesquieu himself would seem to incline to this idea, when, as M. Ducrocq points out, he speaks of the executive power as " la puissance *exécutrice* des choses qui dépendent du droit des gens," and the judicial power as " la puissance exécutrice des choses qui dépendent du droit civil." Ducrocq, *Traité du Droit Administratif*, 6th edition, 1881, Vol. I., p. 29.

[2] See People *v.* Simon, 176 Ill. 165; 68 Am. State Rep. 175.

made the basis of these instruments.   Judge Miller of the United States Supreme Court says :[1] "It is believed to be one of the chief merits of the American system of written constitutional law that all powers intrusted to governments, whether state or national, are divided into the three grand departments of the executive, the legislative, and the judicial ; that the functions appropriate to each of these branches of government shall be vested in a separate body of public servants; and that the perfection of the system requires that the lines which separate and divide these departments shall be broadly and clearly defined.   It is also essential to the successful working of the system that the persons intrusted with power in any one of these branches shall not be permitted to encroach upon the powers confided to the others, but that each shall by the law of its creation be limited to the exercise of the powers appropriate to its own department and no others."

This principle of the separation of powers and authorities has proven, however, to be unworkable as a legal principle.   The courts have made many exceptions to it, all in the direction of recognizing what one of them calls "'a common because of vicinage' bordering on the domains of each" authority, in the occupancy of which each authority must

[1] Kilbourn *v.* Thompson, 103 U. S. 168.

tolerate the others.[1] The principle of the separation of authorities, notwithstanding constitutional
provisions and judicial decisions and *dicta* on the
general subject, must therefore be regarded as
existent in our constitutional law only in an at-
tenuated form.

The frequent exceptions made to the theory of
the separation of authorities are due, however, not
merely to the decisions of the courts. They are
due as well to the constitutions themselves. This
is true both of American and of European constitutions. No political organization, based on the
general theory of a differentiation of governmental
functions, has ever been established which assigns
the function of expressing the will of the state
exclusively to any one of the organs for which it
makes provision.

Thus, the organ of government whose main
function is the execution of the will of the state is
often, and indeed usually, intrusted with the expression of that will in its details. These details,
however, when expressed, must conform with the
general principles laid down by the organ whose
main duty is that of expression. That is, the authority called executive has, in almost all cases,
considerable ordinance or legislative power.

On the other hand, the organ whose main duty

[1] Brown *v.* Turner, 70 N. C. 93, 102.

is to express the will of the state, *i.e.* the legislature, has usually the power to control in one way or another the execution of the state will by that organ to which such execution is in the main intrusted. That is, while the two primary functions of government are susceptible of differentiation, the organs of government to which the discharge of these functions is intrusted cannot be clearly defined.

It is impossible to assign each of these functions to a separate authority, not merely because the exercise of governmental power cannot be clearly apportioned, but also because, as political systems develop, these two primary functions of government tend to be differentiated into minor and secondary functions. The discharge of each of these minor functions is intrusted to somewhat separate and independent governmental organs. These organs have each its own name and place in the governmental system.

Thus, for example, the will of the state as to different matters may be expressed by different state organs. This is a characteristic feature of the American political system, in which the constitution-making authority, that is, the people, expresses the will of the state as to the form of governmental organization and the fundamental rights of the individual; while the legislature, another governmental organ, expresses the will of the state in most cases where it has not been expressed in the constitution. Again, as a result, either of the provisions of the constitution or of the delegation of the power by the legislature, the chief executive or subordinate executive authorities may, through the issue of ordinances, express the will of the state as to details where it is inconvenient for the legislature to act.

The same is true of the execution of the will of the state. If we analyze the organization of any concrete government, we shall find that there are three kinds of authorities which are engaged in the execution of the state will. These are, in the first place, the authorities which apply the law in concrete cases where controversies arise owing to the failure of private individuals or public authorities to observe the rights of others. Such authorities are known as judicial authorities. They are, in the second place, the authorities which have the general supervision of the execution of the state will, and which are commonly referred to as executive authorities. They are, finally, the authorities which are attending to the scientific, technical, and, so to speak, commercial activities of the government, and which are in all countries, where such activities have attained prominence, known as administrative authorities.

As government becomes more complex these three authorities, all of which are engaged in the execution of the will of the state, tend to become more and more differentiated. The first to become so differentiated are the judicial authorities. Not only is this differentiation of the judicial authorities first in point of time, it is also the clearest. Indeed, it is so clear in some instances as to lead many students, as has been pointed out, to mark off the activity of the judicial authorities as a separate power or function of government.

Enough has been said, it is believed, to show that there are two distinct functions of government, and that their differentiation results in a differentiation, though less complete, of the organs of government provided by the formal governmental system. These two functions of government may for purposes of convenience be designated respectively as Politics and Administration. Politics has to do with policies or expressions of the state will. Administration has to do with the execution of these policies.

It is of course true that the meaning which is here given to the word " politics " is not the meaning which has been attributed to that word by most political writers. At the same time it is submitted that the sense in which politics is here used is the sense in which it is used by most people in ordinary affairs. Thus the Century Dictionary defines "politics": "In the narrower and more usual sense, the act or vocation of guiding or influencing the policy of a government through the organization of a party among its citizens — including, therefore, not only the ethics of government, but more especially, and often to the exclusion of ethical principles, the art of influencing public opinion, attracting and marshalling voters, and obtaining and distributing public patronage, so far as the possession of offices may depend upon the political opinions or political services of individuals."

An explanation of the word "administration" is not perhaps so necessary, since in scientific parlance it has not as yet acquired so fixed a meaning as has "politics." Block, in his *Dictionnaire de l'administration française*, defines "administration" as: "L'ensemble des services publiques destinés à concourir à l'exécution de la pensée du gouvernement et à l'application des lois d'intérêt general." The Century Dictionary speaks of it as: "The duty or duties of the administrator; specifically, the executive functions of government, consisting in the exercise of all the powers and duties of government, both general and local, which are neither legislative nor judicial."

These definitions, it will be noticed, both lay

stress upon the fact that politics has to do with the
guiding or influencing of governmental policy, while
administration has to do with the execution of that
policy.   It is these two functions which it is here
desired to differentiate, and for which the words
" politics " and " administration " have been chosen.

The use of the word "administration" in this connection is unfortunately somewhat misleading, for
the word when accompanied by the definite article
is also used to indicate a series of governmental
authorities.   " The administration " means popularly the most important executive or administrative authorities. "Administration," therefore, when
used as indicative of function, is apt to promote
the idea that this function of government is to be
found exclusively in the work of what are commonly referred to as executive or administrative
authorities.   These in their turn are apt to be
regarded as confined to the discharge of the function of administration.   Such, however, is rarely
the case in any political system, and is particularly
not the case in the American governmental system.   The American legislature discharges very
frequently the function of administration through
its power of passing special acts.   The American
executive has an important influence on the discharge of the function of politics through the
exercise of its veto power.

Further, in the United States, the words "administration" and "administrative," as indicative of governmental function, are commonly used by the courts in a very loose way. The attempt was made at the time of the formation of our governmental system, as has been pointed out, to incorporate into it the principle of the separation of powers. What had been a somewhat nebulous theory of political science thus became a rigid legal doctrine. What had been a somewhat attractive political theory in its nebulous form became at once an unworkable and unapplicable rule of law.

To avoid the inconvenience resulting from the attempt made to apply it logically to our governmental system, the judges of the United States have been accustomed to call "administrative" any power which was not in their eyes exclusively and unqualifiedly legislative, executive, or judicial, and to permit such a power to be exercised by any authority.[1]

While this habit on the part of the judges makes the selection of the word "administration" somewhat unfortunate; at the same time it is indicative of the fact to which attention has been more than once directed, that although the differentiation of two functions of government is clear,

[1] Bondy, "Separation of Governmental Powers," *Columbia College Series in History, Economics, and Public Law*, Vol. V., p. 202 *et seq.*

the assignment of such functions to separate authorities is impossible.

Finally, the different position assigned in different states to the organ to which most of the work of executing the will of the state has been intrusted, has resulted in quite different conceptions in different states of what has been usually called administration.   For administration has been conceived of as the function of the executing, that is, the executive authority.   Recently, however, writers on administration have seen that, from the point of view both of theoretical speculation and of practical expediency, administration should not be regarded as merely a function of the executive authority, that is, the authority in the government which by the positive law is the executing authority.   It has been seen that administration is, on the contrary, the function of executing the will of the state.   It may be in some respects greater, and in others less in extent than the function of the executing authority as determined by the positive law.

There are, then, in all governmental systems two primary or ultimate functions of government, viz. the expression of the will of the state and the execution of that will.   There are also in all states separate organs, each of which is mainly busied with the discharge of one of these functions.   These functions are, respectively, Politics and Administration.

CHAPTER II

THE function of politics, it has been shown, consists in the expression of the will of the state. Its discharge may not, however, be intrusted exclusively to any authority or any set of authorities in the government. Nor on the other hand may any authority or set of authorities be confined exclusively to its discharge. The principle of the separation of powers in its extreme form cannot, therefore, be made the basis of any concrete political organization. For this principle demands that there shall be separate authorities of the government, each of which shall be confined to the discharge of one of the functions of government which are differentiated. Actual political necessity however requires that there shall be harmony between the expression and execution of the state will.

Lack of harmony between the law and its execution results in political paralysis. A rule of conduct, *i.e.* an expression of the state will, practically amounts to nothing if it is not executed. It is a mere *brutum fulmen.* On the other hand the execution of a rule of conduct which is not the expression of the state will is really an exercise by the executing authority of the right to express the state will.

Now in order that this harmony between the expression and the execution of the state will may be obtained, the independence either of the body which expresses the state will or of the body which executes it must be sacrificed. Either the executing authority must be subordinated to the expressing authority, or the expressing authority must be subjected to the control of the executing authority. Only in this way will there be harmony in the government. Only in this way can the expression of the real state will become an actual rule of conduct generally observed.

Finally, popular government requires that it is the executing authority which shall be subordinated to the expressing authority, since the latter in the nature of things can be made much more representative of the people than can the executing authority.

In other words, practical political necessity makes impossible the consideration of the function of politics apart from that of administration. Politics must have a certain control over administration, using the words in the broad senses heretofore attributed to them. That some such relation must exist between the two ultimate functions of government is seen when we examine the political development of any state.

If, in the hope of preventing politics from influencing administration in its details, the attempt is made to provide for the legal separation of the bodies in the government mainly charged with these two functions respectively, the tendency is for the necessary control to develop extra-legally. This is the case in the American political system.

The American political system is largely based on the fundamental principle of the separation of governmental powers. It has been impossible for the necessary control of politics over administration to develop within the formal governmental system on account of the independent position assigned by the constitutional law to executive and administrative officers. The control has therefore developed in the party system. The American political party busies itself as much with the election of administrative and executive officers as it does with the election of bodies recognized as distinctly political in character, as having to do with the expression of the state will. The party system thus secures that harmony between the functions of politics and administration which must exist if government is to be carried on successfully.[1]

On the other hand, if no attempt is made in the governmental system to provide for the separation of politics and administration, and if the governmental institutions are not put into comparatively unyielding and inflexible form through the adoption of a written constitution, the control and superintendence of the function of administration tends to be assumed by the governmental body which discharges the political function.

Thus, in England, after the people had got into their hands the control of the expression of the will of the state through their control of Parliament, they at once set to work to have Parliament, their representative, recognized as having a control over the authorities of government to which was intrusted the execution of the will of the state. In this they have succeeded. The result is the present system of ministerial responsibility to Parliament.

While the function of politics has to do, therefore, primarily with the expression of the state will, it has to do secondarily with the execution of that will.

[1] Mr. H. J. Ford in his book entitled *The Rise and Growth of American Politics*, a most valuable and interesting work, is the first writer to call attention to the fact that this most important duty has been assumed by the political party in the American system of government.

So far as it has to do with the expression of the state will, its ramifications are most extended. Thus the function of politics has to do with the determination of the question who ultimately and who secondarily and derivatively shall express the will of the state. That is, it has to solve problems of sovereignty and problems of government. It must define, in a representative political system, who are the voters, how and for whom they shall vote, and what authorities in the governmental system shall make the law.

The consideration of such questions, further, involves something more than the consideration of the organization of the formal government. It involves also the consideration of the organization of the parties through whose action the choice of voters is limited to the few persons for whom they vote, and the principles of political action are determined upon. For the organization provided for this purpose has just as much to do with the expression of the will of the people as has the formal governmental organization. A popular, representative form of government with an autocratic party organization controlled by an oligarchy or a party despot may not result in as really a popular political system, *i.e.* may not permit of as ready an expression of the popular or state will, as a less popular form of government combined with a less autocratic form of party organization.

The student of the function of politics who would deal intelligently with his subject must, therefore, consider the party system where that has become so important as to exercise an influence on the governmental system.[1]

Sometimes the party becomes so important as to be made a part of the formal governmental system, and to receive legal recognition. The United States offers a good example on this point. In our early political history the law had almost nothing to say about the method of elections, and absolutely nothing about the organization and action of parties. Parties had, however, developed in some of the colonies previous to the Revolution, and in one of the colonies, viz. New York, the struggle between them had already begun to evidence some of the bitterness which has always since that time characterized the politics of that state.[2]

The bitterness of party strife resulted in the insertion in the first constitution of the state of a provision that the vote should be by ballot, *i.e.*

[1] Mr. Lowell's recent and most excellent work on *Government and Parties in Continental Europe* is a shining example of the value of the study of parties to the student of government.

[2] Gitterman, "Council of Appointment in New York," *Political Science Quarterly*, Vol. VII., 1892, p. 80.

secret. The ballot has since become an essential part of our electoral system. With the increase in the number of voters and in the number of elective officers, the mere provision for a ballot was not regarded as sufficient. Statute after statute has been passed regulating the form and appearance of the ballot. These statutes have been enforced with great rigor by the courts. All ballots which have not conformed to the law and whose failure to conform thereto would result in revealing the voter's identity have been thrown out as illegal and ineffective. The whole purpose of this legislation was, by securing a secret vote, to prevent the party organizations from making use of what had come to be regarded as illegitimate means of persuading the voters to support particular candidates.

Before, however, this legislation had been completed it had been found that, in states where the work of the party was greatest, party competition had resulted in attempts at "repeating" as it was called, *i.e.* in one voter's voting more than once for the same candidate; in "colonization," *i.e.* in the voting of unqualified persons who were massed together in election districts under the supervision of the party leaders; and of ballot-box stuffing and false counting. To remedy these evils the system of registering the voters was adopted, and provisions were inserted in the election law whose purpose was to secure an honest count.

Finally it appeared that altogether too great a burden was by the general electoral system devolved upon the party, owing to the fact that the printing and distribution of the ballots were not undertaken by the government.   It was practically impossible for any organization not possessed of great financial strength to do the work previous to elections which was necessary to nominate candidates and keep them in the field.[1]   Provision was, therefore, made for the printing and distribution of the ballots by state officers and at state expense, in general, in accordance with methods adopted first in Australia.

The Australian system of voting was known to us mainly from the English Ballot Act of 1872, into which it had been incorporated.   This system was, however, formed for a political system which did not make the demands upon the political party which are made by the American political system. The number of voters was considerably less in England than in the United States.   The number of officers to be elected at a single election in England was incomparably smaller than here.   On this account the demand was at once made that the

[1] See Ivins, *Money in Elections*.

Australian system should be altered to suit American conditions.

The main point in which alteration of the English ballot law was demanded was in the qualifications necessary to secure recognition on the official ballot. The English election law provided that candidates should have their names printed on the official ballot after they had been put in formal nomination by a small number of voters. It further provided, in accordance with old English precedents, that in case only one such formal nomination was made the candidate so nominated should be declared elected by the returning officer without the formality of a poll. Finally, every candidate was obliged to pay the expenses occasioned by the printing of his name on the ballot.

Several things must be noticed in this English system of voting. In the first place, the party as such received no legal recognition whatever. There was no necessity for such recognition because the work devolved upon the party was very slight. As a general thing only one position was to be filled at each election. The provision that a poll was not in all cases necessary made it unnecessary for each party to name a candidate at each election. It was therefore unnecessary and often inexpedient for each party to keep up a permanent organization. Such a permanent organization, further, was for a long time not so necessary as here because of the smaller number of voters to be influenced. Finally, the provision that each candidate should pay for printing his name on the official ballot, when a poll was to be taken, tended to prevent the parties from putting up candidates where their chances of election were not reasonably good.

The English Ballot Act was, therefore, from the point of view of theory, not suited to the United States, where the political conditions were so different, unless important modifications were made in it. The modifications which were very generally made consisted largely in the legal recognition by the state of the political parties as nominating agencies.

The legal recognition of parties was accomplished in one of two ways, and generally in both. In the first place, the certificate of a party convention was required for a regular party nomination. In many instances, in addition, the candidates of each party were printed on the ballot in one column, either under a title, stating the name of the party, or under an emblem, formally chosen by the party, which should be sufficient to indicate to illiterate voters the party to which such candidates belonged. Finally, in the new laws based upon the principle of the Australian system, the party was generally defined as a political organization which had cast a certain percentage of the vote at the last election.

In all the states which adopted this system it will be noticed that some legal recognition of the party as a political organ was made. Most of the states adopted the party column ballot. It has frequently been urged that the adoption of the party column ballot was due to the desire of party managers to make difficult, or at any rate to discourage, political action independent of party. It must, however, be remembered that such action is made difficult if not impossible by the American system of government. The American electoral system makes such demands on the elector that, in order to meet them, he must of necessity rely on the party. He cannot be expected without its aid to select from among the candidates put in nomination for the numerous offices to be filled by election the individuals for whom he desires to cast his vote.

In the thickly populated districts where the voting population is large and not very intelligent, and the officers to be chosen at one election are many in number, the ordinary voter must, in the nature of things, rely very much on the work of the parties previous to the election. He cannot, in districts where the feeling of neighborhood is not strong, be expected to know much about the personal merits and demerits of the candidates.

Again, it is important, if harmony in government is desirable, that all the candidates of one or the other of the great parties in a given administrative district should be elected. The individual candidates must be sunk to a large extent in the party. Individual responsibility must give place to party responsibility.

In order, however, that voters should not be confined to action with the regular recognized parties, and that new parties might come into existence as necessity might require, provision was made for nomination by certificate. Often, however, the number of persons required to make a nomination through the method of nomination by certificate, was so large as to make this method extremely difficult of application. The number necessary to make an independent nomination was purposely made large for the same reasons for which the party column was adopted, and because it was deemed necessary to prevent inconsiderate nominations. The ballots were printed at public expense, not as in England at the expense of the candidates.

This brief sketch of the development of our election and ballot laws shows, then, both that the study of the party system becomes often a necessity to the student of the function of politics, and that in the United States the party has gradually been recognized by the law. The party has thus taken its place in our formal governmental organization.

But the function of politics has to do not merely with the determination of who shall express the will of the state. It has also to do with the determination of the methods in which this will shall be expressed. Thus it may be the case that in a particular state particular formalities are provided for the expression of the will of the state with regard to particular matters. It is often the case that the will of the state with regard to the form of government is expressed in a particular way quite different from that in which the will of the state is expressed relative to current matters of governmental routine. The methods of expressing the will of the state in reference to the form of government, are generally of such a character as to demand of the persons or authorities to whom the formal expression of the will of the state is intrusted, greater deliberateness of action. The same is true very often of what are regarded as the fundamental rights of the individual members of the state. We find thus in the United States a difference in the methods of constitution-making and of legislation. For the former, the action of a special governmental organ, the constitutional convention, and of the people as a whole is often necessary. For the latter, the action of a legislative body alone is sufficient.

Where organs, which for the most part are acting in the execution of the state will, have the power to determine in concrete cases whether the provisions of the constitution are complied with by the legislature, such organs become in their exercise of this power constitutional, and therefore political organs. The courts in the United States have the power to determine whether an act passed by the legislature is constitutional. The courts thus aid in the expression of the will of the state, and are therefore organs for the discharge of the function of politics, in the sense in which that word is used in these pages.

It has been said that the function of politics, while having to do primarily with the expression of the will of the state, has also to do secondarily with its execution. For there must be harmony between the expression and the execution of the state will, *i.e.* between the making and enforcement of law. It has also been said, that in a popular government the body which expresses the state will or makes the law, must have some control over the body which executes such state will or law. Finally, it has been shown that such necessary control may be found either in the formal governmental system, or outside of that system and in the political party.

Whether this control be found in or outside of the governmental system, its existence is necessitated by the fact, that without it orderly and progressive government is impossible. It should, therefore, extend so far as is necessary to produce that harmony between the expression and the execution of the state will which has been shown to be so necessary. If, however, it is extended beyond this limit, it at once loses its *raison d'être*. This control may be made use of, for example, to perpetuate the existence of a particular party organization, instead of serving as a means to aid in bringing it about that a given expression of the state will shall become an actual rule of conduct. If such use is made of this control, it becomes a means whereby the spontaneous expression by the people of the popular will is actually prevented. Such an exercise of the necessary control of politics over administration introduces an artificial, unnatural element into the problem of securing an expression of the state will. It tends to make the formal expression of the state will opposed to what is the actual state will.

Too greatly extending this necessary control, therefore, really defeats the purpose for which it is

formed.   Not only is this the case, but as will be
pointed out later, too greatly extending this control tends to hamper the efficient discharge of the
function of administration.   For that function is,
under the exercise of this too greatly extended
control, discharged not so much with reference to
the execution of an already expressed state will as
with reference to influencing the future expression
of the state will, *i.e.* in the interest of a political
party or social class.

While, therefore, in the interest of securing the
execution of the state will, politics should have a
control over administration, in the interest both of
popular government and efficient administration,
that control should not be permitted to extend
beyond the limits necessary in order that the
legitimate purpose of its existence be fulfilled.

The tendency of the body in the state possessing the power to express the state will is, however,
always to make use of its powers of control over
the execution of the state will in such a way as to
influence improperly the expression of the state
will.   This is done sometimes from the purest and
most patriotic motives, but more frequently from
vicious and selfish motives.   In either case the
result is apt to be the same.   The law ceases to
be administered impartially, and is administered
solely or largely in the hope of influencing directly

or indirectly the future expression of the state will, and frequently in the interest of certain classes in the community.

The evils arising from the partial and interested administration of the law are so great that the most progressive political communities have felt obliged to take a long step toward securing the independence of certain of the authorities intrusted with the administration of the law. Such, for example, has been the case in England, which, from a very early time, has based her governmental system on the principle that no rule of conduct, *i.e.* no expression of the state will, should be enforced until the concurrence of some authority independent of the authority laying down such rule of conduct had been obtained. Such a statement of the principle underlying the English governmental system must not be understood as meaning that the system of enforcing the law may not at any time be changed. It means merely that in so far as the authorities which enforce or execute the state will are independent of the authority expressing that will, the system actually provides that the concurrence of the executing body must be obtained before an expression of the will of the state becomes an actual rule of conduct.

The influence of this principle may be seen in all branches of the English public law. It is naturally the most marked in the case of the administration of justice, because it is most necessary that justice be administered impartially, *i.e.* without regard to the interests of the individual claimants before the court, and with as little regard as possible to the effect the particular decision will have upon the future expression of the will of the state.

The original English system of administering justice assigned to the courts an extremely independent position. Indeed, the original English courts, on account of their popular character, not only executed the law ; they made the law. With the growth of the royal power, however, judges were appointed by the Crown. They strove, as far as in them lay, to get into their hands the determination of questions of law, *i.e.* the expression of the state will, and to relegate the jury, the popular element of the courts which was retained, to the application of the law, as laid down by the judge, to the facts as found by them, *i.e.* to the execution of the state will. But the jury were able, notwithstanding the efforts of the judges, to retain in their own hands the power to acquit a prisoner brought before them, and their judgment of acquittal was not subject to review by any court or authority whatsoever.[1]

[1] See the famous case of Lieutenant-Colonel Lilburne, who, being banished by Parliament and being brought to trial for re-

While the courts, leaving aside the jury system, have never been in England legally independent of Parliament, the body expressing in the main the will of the state, public opinion does not recognize that it is proper for that body to exercise any con-

turning to England, was acquitted by a jury, on the ground that the act of Parliament banishing him was illegal, the jury thus claiming that it was the judge of the law as well as the facts, notwithstanding the charge of the judge to the contrary, 12 Harggrave's State Trials, 79, 80. See also Penn and Mead's Trials, 6 Howell's State Trials, 992, where a committee of the House of Commons reported that the proceedings of the chief justice, who had fined jurors for not convicting a prisoner in accordance with his directions, were "innovations in the trial of men for their lives and liberties, and that he had used an arbitrary and illegal power, which was of dangerous consequence to the lives and liberties of the people of England and tends to the introducing of arbitrary government." See also Bushel's case, Vaughan, 135–158, where a juror committed for refusing to follow the charge of a judge was released on *habeas corpus*. The rule is the same in the United States. See Wharton, 5 Southern Law Review, 355, cited in note to 33 Amer. Rep. 791; Kane *v.* Commonwealth, 89 Pa. St. 522 ; 33 Amer. Rep. 787, where Chief Justice Sharswood says: "It has been strongly contended that, though the jury have the power, they have not the right to give a verdict contrary to the instruction of the court upon the law. In other words, that to do so would be a breach of their duty and a violation of their oaths. The distinction between power and right, whatever may be its value in ethics, in law is very shadowy and unsubstantial. He who has legal power has legal right." See also Judge Hall's opinion, in State *v.* Croteau, 23 Vermont, 14; 54 Amer. Dec. 90, where it is said: "The power of juries to decide the law as well as the facts involved in the issue of 'not guilty' and without legal responsibility to any other tribunal for their decision is universally conceded. In my opinion, such power is equivalent to right."

trol over their actions in the interest of influencing in any way the future action of Parliament. While legally the courts are thus not independent, politically they are.

In the United States we have, however, made the judges legally independent of the legislature except in the one respect that they are subject to impeachment; and all attempts to rob them of their independence over against the body back of the legislatures, *i.e.* the political party, meet with very general reprobation.

It may be said, therefore, that English speaking peoples have come to the conclusion that the danger of permitting distinctly political bodies to exercise a control over the administration of justice is so great, that the authorities entrusted with this branch of the execution of the state will should be vested with very great independence, even at the risk of depriving the expressed will of the state of its quality of being actually a rule of conduct.

The English rule, that the concurrence of some authority independent of the body expressing the will of the state must be obtained before the expression of the state will should become an actual rule of conduct, was adopted as well in the administration of government as in the administration of justice. It was applied most prominently in the system of local government for which England has been celebrated.

The English system of local government was characterized by the great independence of the local administrative authorities intrusted with the enforcement of law. It was due to this system that the Stuarts were unable to establish the system of absolute government for which they struggled so desperately and so long.

This system of local government, also, was introduced into the United States, where, again, as was the case with the principle of judicial independence, it received a greater legal development than in the land of its birth. While, however, the administrative system of the United States was, owing to the adoption of the English local government system and to that of the principle of the separation of powers, put legally in a very independent position over against the body intrusted with the legal expression of the state will, *i.e.* the legislature, it has, as a matter of fact, been subjected to the control of the political party. The result has been that actually administration has been subjected too much to the control of politics in the United States. This has had the effect of decreasing administrative efficiency. It has also brought it about that the administrative system is made use of to influence the expression of the state will, and sometimes to cause the formal expression of the state will to be at variance with the real state will. This must inevitably be the case where the control of the political body over the administrative body is carried beyond its proper limits as already outlined.

What has been said must not be understood as meaning that the administrative system should be as completely removed from political control as the courts. Such a claim could not be for a moment admitted. For the execution of law, the expressed will of the state, depends in a large degree upon the active initiative of the administrative authorities. They should be subjected to political control to the end that they take such initiative. Such is not the case with the courts, which are called upon merely to execute the law on the application of individuals.

It is, however, true that the control of politics over what has been called the administration of government should not be carried beyond the limits indicated ; and that, if so carried, the consequences upon the general efficiency of the administration in the execution of the state will, and the ability of the people to express that will, will inevitably be disastrous.

The undue extension of politics over the administration of government may be prevented, indeed has been in the past prevented, by recognizing a degree of independence in the administrative as in the judicial authorities. It can also be secured by the cultivation of a sound public opinion. This, it has been pointed out, is the great protection of the judicial authorities in both England and the United States. Further, it is the only protection which can be offered to either the judicial or the administrative authorities against the exercise of political influences by bodies such as political parties, not occupying a well-defined position in the formal governmental system, but still holding a position of the greatest importance in the extra-governmental — political — system.

Our analysis of the function of politics thus leads us to the conclusion, that it has to do both with the expression and the execution of the state will — with the former primarily, with the latter secondarily. This function of politics further embraces constitution making, legislation, the selection of governmental officers, and the control of the function of executing the will of the state. A function so complex as that of politics cannot be discharged by any particular governmental authority, or any particular set of governmental authorities.

While we may say in a general way that, so far as the discharge of the function of politics consists in the making and amending of the constitution, it is discharged by the constitutional convention, we must remember that the authority interpreting the constitution also discharges it. In the American system of government, this authority is very commonly the judicial authority.

Again, we may say that so far as the exercise of the function of politics consists in legislation, it is discharged by the legislature. But we must remember that the executive authority, and in many instances local authorities, have a power of ordinance. The exercise of this power of ordinance results in decrees which can with difficulty be distinguished from legislation. Courts also through the power of judicial decision often make law.

Finally, we must remember that the action of the constitutional convention, and to a lesser degree that of the courts, the legislature, and the executive and local authorities, may be and often are controlled by an extra-governmental body, the political party, whose organization and whose conduct have thus an important, if not a controlling, influence on the discharge of the function of politics.

CHAPTER III

ALL states are based more or less on the federal idea. That is, all states are made up of local communities which in many instances have their own needs separate from the needs of the state as a whole. Further, all states of any size must be divided into districts in which matters of purely state concern are attended to. As a general thing, the local communities are chosen as the districts for certain, though not for all, the purposes of state government. Thus, in the older parts of the United States, the town, which is a natural growth, is not merely a local corporation with, in many cases, its own property and its own liabilities separate and distinct from the property and the liabilities of the state as a whole. It is also a district for such purposes of state government as the administration of justice and the assessment and collection of state taxes. The same is true of most of the cities, and particularly of the larger cities. They are at the same time local communities and state administrative districts.

In attending to its own concerns, such a local

47

community is, so to speak, a state in miniature. That is, like the state, it has a will to express and execute. If it were possible to assign to the local community its sphere of action, and to the state its sphere of action, each might express and execute its will irrespective of each other. But such delimitation is impossible. Either the state or the local community must be supreme. That is, in case of conflict as to whether a given matter is within the sphere of local or of state action, such conflict must be decided finally either by the state or by the local community. If it is the former which has the power of decision, the government may be made a very centralized one, as a result of the decision by the state of all conflicts in its own favor. On the other hand, if it is the local community which has the power of decision, the result of its exercise of this power in favor of itself may be state disintegration.

Where a written constitution is adopted, which is to be interpreted by the courts, the attempt may be made to delimit the spheres of state and local competence in that instrument. Much good will unquestionably result from such an attempt; but here again, it must be remembered that the courts which are to interpret the constitution must be either state or local courts, and will be influenced in their decisions by the fact of their origin as well as by the prevalent political thought. For these questions are really political rather than legal in character. Public opinion, further, will in many cases, without the intervention of a written constitution, do much to prevent too great centralization and to check a too marked tendency toward state disintegration.

Moreover, the administrative system, which is itself, of course, a product of public opinion, has an important influence on this problem. The administrative system is that part of the governmental organization which has primarily to do with the execution of the will of the state. It has been pointed out that no expression of the will of the state is anything more than an empty phrase if the body which expresses it has no control over its execution. The theory of the government may recognize the subordination to the state of the local community so far as the expression of the will of the state is concerned. The administrative system may, however, be so arranged as to make the actual practice quite the contrary of the theory. The expression of the state will may be intrusted to an organ of the state central government. If, however, the actual execution of the state will is intrusted to the local community free from any effective state control, such local community may, through its powers of execution, or what are really powers of non-execution or modification, change the will of the state as expressed by the body representing the state as a whole, so as to adapt it to what are believed to be the needs of the local community.

This is the actual condition of things where, while legislation is centralized, the administration of that legislation is decentralized or localized. This is the most important characteristic of what we are accustomed to call local self-government. Such a method of administration, as we see it in the countries which have adopted it, like England and the states of the United States, starts out with the proposition that the state is sovereign over all the local communities of which it is composed. The state may not, and in many cases does not, recognize any local will which is capable of expression by the local communities. It may, and often does, regulate in such detail the powers of local communities as to leave them little opportunity to exercise any discretion. It does, however, grant to such local communities most important powers of executing state laws practically free from any effective state control.

The result of such a system of local self-government is that state laws which are unpopular in specific communities are often not enforced, or are enforced with such modifications as to make the same law quite different as a rule of conduct in different parts of the state. Thus, in 1850, the state of New York passed a law providing that there should be established in each town a board of health. Very little was done, however, by the towns for more than thirty years toward the establishment of such boards, and it was only after the establishment in 1880 of a State Board of Health with power to insist upon the observance of the law that the law was obeyed.[1]

Such a method of regulating the relations of the state and local communities is, of course, illogical. But it unquestionably does provide, though indirectly, for an expression of the local will on matters which seem of importance to the local communities without endangering the theoretical sovereignty of the state, and without attempting to enter upon that most difficult problem, the differentiation of the spheres of state and local action. At the same time, it makes impossible the execution of the state will, where that will is opposed by the local will, and has, therefore, to be abandoned where unity of purpose and harmony of action throughout the entire state are necessary.

[1] Fairlie, "The Centralization of Administration in New York," *Columbia University Series in History,* etc., Vol. IX., No. 3, p. 124–133.

Opposed to local self-government as above described, we find administrative centralization. While local self-government is usually accompanied by considerable legislative decentralization, administrative centralization is often accompanied by considerable legislative decentralization. That is, where the will of the state is expressed altogether or mainly by a central state organ, its execution is intrusted very largely to local communities independent from the administrative point of view; and where the execution of the state will is in the hands of the central government of the state, it is not infrequently the case that the local communities have large powers of expressing the local will free from state control.

As opposed, then, to local self-government as we see it in the United States, administrative centralization as we see it on the Continent distinguishes more clearly a sphere of local action, giving the local communities greater powers of action in expressing the local will, and reserving to the state greater powers of executing its own will. Under a system of administrative centralization local communities may exist, but are seldom made agents for the execution of state laws. The local community has its own sphere of action and its own organs for the expression of its own will.

The state has its own administrative system centrally appointed and centrally controlled.

Further, whereas, under a system of local self-government, it is the legislature which exercises the central control over the local communities, in that it delimits their competence often in such a way as to leave them little power to express the local will at all, under a system of administrative centralization, such central control as is exercised over the local communities is exercised, not by the legislature, but by the body intrusted with the most important administrative functions, *i.e.* the chief executive authority.

Administrative centralization, finally, is in most cases characterized by the fact that centrally appointed officials have in their hands the execution of policies which, by the law, are recognized as distinctly local. Thus, in France, the home of administrative centralization, the prefect, appointed by the chief executive, and the mayor, who acts under the control of the prefect, are respectively the chief administrative officers of the most important local communities, the department and the commune, *i.e.* are the officers who are to execute the local will. Under the system of local self-government, locally selected and locally controlled officers execute state laws. Under the system of administrative centralization centrally selected or centrally controlled officers frequently execute local policies.

In the local self-government system of administration, the theoretical failure to recognize any local will is, to a degree, offset by the actual existence of local power to execute or not to execute the state will. In the systems of administrative centralization with which we are acquainted, the theoretical recognition of the local will is often offset by the actual execution of that local will by officers subject to central control. Local self-government tends to sacrifice the interests of the state in that it makes difficult, if not impossible, the execution of the state will, where there is a conflict between the state and a local community. Administrative centralization sacrifices the interests of the local community, in that it does not make sufficient provision for the execution by local agents of the local will. Neither system thus produces those harmonious relations between the state and the local communities which are so necessary for efficient and harmonious government.

On this account, the tendency of those countries which have adopted most completely the system of local self-government is to abandon it for a régime of centralized administration where the execution of the state will is felt to be absolutely necessary. On the other hand, the tendency of states in which the régime of administrative centralization has been adopted is to recognize greater powers of local autonomy in those cases where local expression and local execution of the local will seem advisable, and where they can be provided without endangering the unity of the state.

England, the home of local self-government, has during the last century been fast centralizing her administrative system. The states of the United States, where local self-government has received its greatest development, have within the last fifty years been taking steps in the same direction.[1] England has been gradually differentiating a sphere of distinctly state action. The states of the United States also have been forming, for the new branches of administration made necessary by the increasing complexity and variety of modern civilized life, an administrative system entirely within the control of the central government of the state.

Both England and the states of the United States have been in greater or less degree subjecting local communities, so far as they are per-

[1] Maltbie, "English Local Government of To-day," *Col. Univ. Pub.*, Vol. IX., No. 1. Fairlie, *op. cit.* Whitten, "Public Administration in Massachusetts," *Col. Univ. Pub.*, Vol. VIII., No. 4.

mitted to execute state laws, to the control of state administrative authorities. In England large powers of supervision over the actions of the local communities have been given to the Local Government Board, the Education Department and the Treasury. In the United States similar powers have been given to State Superintendents of Common Schools or similar officers, and State Boards of Health, Charities, and Equalization.

While both England and the states of the United States have thus been centralizing their administrative system in order to attain the efficient execution of the will of the state, France and Germany, where the administration has in the past been highly centralized, have been decentralizing their administrative systems by establishing local corporations with large powers of local action and of choosing their own officers, in the hope of securing the expression and execution by the local communities of the local will.[1]

The attempt thus being made both in the United States and Europe to differentiate a local from the state will, and to secure its expression and execution by the local communities, would seem in several important respects to have been more successful in Europe than in the United States. This is cer-

[1] Goodnow, *Comparative Administrative Law*, I, 271, 300, and authorities cited.

tainly true so far as the positive expression of the
local will is concerned. This success is due, it is
believed, to the following causes :

It has been pointed out that the original Anglo-
American system of local self-government was
based on the theory that the will of the state —
hardly any local will being recognized — was to be
expressed by state and seldom by local organs;
but that this will, once expressed, was to be executed by local organs. Local communities were
thus able to exercise a sort of veto power by electing officers who would refuse to execute the will of
the state.

Local communities could not, however, through
their powers of non-execution take any positive
action. For their powers of action were enumerated in state legislation. If they wanted more
power, they had to apply to the legislature for it.
The centralization of administration, which, it has
been pointed out, has been going on during the
century that is now closing, while it has done much
to insure the execution of the will of the state in
matters of interest to the state as a whole, has not,
however, of itself enlarged in any way the powers
of the local communities in the expression of the
local will.

The attempt has, it is true, been made in the
United States to secure greater local autonomy

by limiting the power of the legislature over the local communities. Many provisions of this sort have been inserted into the state constitutions. Some of these, such as those assuring to localities the right to select their own officers, tend however, where these officers have simply executive powers, merely to emphasize the local self-government character of the administrative system as it has been described. Other provisions, such as those which positively forbid action by the legislature with regard to the local matters of single local communities, do of course impliedly leave the decision of such matters with the local communities.

This prohibition of special legislation relative to localities has, however, been ineffective in securing the expression by the local communities of the local will for two reasons.

In the first place, local communities cannot with due regard to the interests of the state as a whole be removed entirely from the control of the state. State disintegration would follow if this were done. Now if the legislative control, which is the only state control in a local self-government system of administration, were done away with without providing some other means of control, the local communities would be entirely relieved from state control. Both the legislatures and the courts have felt the force of this consideration. The legislatures have often refused, therefore, to abandon their habit of enumerating in detail the powers of local communities, and have passed general acts which were merely general in the sense of applying formally to more than one local community.

But under the system of enumerated local powers, few localities can be governed by general acts applicable to all other similar localities. The pressure upon the legislature for modifications and amendments of these so-called general acts in the interest of particular localities has been therefore almost as great since, as prior to, the adoption of the constitutional provisions prohibiting special legislation. To this pressure the legislature has been obliged to yield. It has done so through the adoption of the device of the classification of localities, the classification actually adopted being in many cases so minute that only one local community is to be found in the class.[1]

The courts when called upon to determine upon the constitutionality of such action have felt obliged to uphold it, since they recognized that without such action local development was impossible.[2] An-

[1] See Wilcox, " Municipal Government in Michigan and Ohio," *Columbia College Series of Studies in History, Economics, and Public Law*, Vol. V., p. 72, *et. seq.;* Goodnow, *Municipal Problems*, p. 41.

[2] See Wheeler *v.* Pennsylvania, 77 Pennsylvania State 332.

other reason why the courts adopted this view is probably to be found in the fact that they recognized as falling under the term "local affairs," as to which special legislation was prohibited, many matters such as police and the administration of justice, which in other branches of the law were regarded as of state rather than local concern.[1] They were léd to this decision by historical considerations. From the historical point of view such matters were local, since they had from time immemorial been attended to, so far as their execution was concerned, by the local communities. Such being the case, a strict construction of the constitutional provisions prohibiting special legislation with regard to local matters would really have resulted in the destruction of all state control over many matters over which state control was absolutely necessary.

Convinced of the inefficiency of the method of constitutional prohibition of special legislation in securing to local communities the expression and execution of the local will, some states attempted not merely to forbid special legislation relative to local affairs, but to take from the legislature and give to those localities whose rights had been most persistently violated by the legislature (*i.e.* the larger cities) the right to regulate their own affairs

[1] Goodnow, *Municipal Home Rule*, p. 77.

free from all state control. This was done in Missouri in 1875. The constitution adopted in that year provided (Art. 9) that the larger cities might draw up their own charters as to their local government, which charters could not be amended nor interfered with in any way by the state legislature.[1] California soon followed suit, but permitted amendment by the legislature in general laws. The California method was as unsuccessful as the prohibition of special legislation had been unsuccessful before; and in 1896 the constitution was so amended as to make it practically the same as that of Missouri.[2] Similar provisions are found in the constitutions of Washington and Minnesota.

This method of securing to the local communities the expression and execution of local will has had more success than any other adopted in the United States. The courts of Missouri have, however, when called upon to interpret the meaning of the constitution as to " local matters," given a much narrower meaning to the term than had previously been given in deciding what were local affairs as to which special legislation was prohibited.[3] Here,

[1] St. Louis *v.* Dorr, 145 Mo. 466 ; 68 Amer. State Reports 575.

[2] See Moffett: " Referendum in the United States," *Political Science Quarterly*, March, 1898.

[3] See article by F. W. Dewart on " The Municipal Condition of St. Louis " in *Louisville Conference for Good City Government*, p. 220.

however, as in the case of the decision of what was special legislation, the courts have been obliged to consider the interests of the state as a whole, and have not been willing to adopt a view which would result in breaking up the state by releasing localities from all state control over matters of interest to the state.

The second reason why constitutional provisions attempting to secure to local governments the expression and execution of the local will have not had the success which was anticipated from them is to be found in the partisan political system obtaining in the United States. For reasons which will be pointed out later this system has developed an extraordinary strength. This party system has been formed primarily to attend to national and state politics, that is to facilitate the expression and execution of the will of the nation and of the state as a whole. This was so because the great political questions which we as a people have been called upon to solve have been national and state questions. The state and national parties, having thus important national and state questions to solve, have not scrupled to sacrifice the interests of the local communities to what they considered to be the interests of the state and nation. They not only have made use of the powers of the legislature over the localities in the interest of the state and nation, but also, by emphasizing the importance of national and state questions on the occasion of local elections, have drowned by their clamor the voices of those individuals who have attempted to call attention to the rights and interests of the local communities.

In acting thus, the political parties have unquestionably in many cases been right. They have been right because under our system of decentralized administration, our local self-government, the localities are in almost all cases important agencies of state government, since they have in their hands the uncontrolled administration of state laws. The state party, formed for the furtherance of issues affecting the welfare of the state as a whole, is of necessity bound to interest itself in local politics. A prohibition party, for example, which had succeeded in placing upon the statute book a law prohibiting the sale of liquor, would fail in its duty if it did not strive to secure control of the government of a city which had in its hands, not subject to an effective state control, the management of the police which was to enforce such prohibition law. Now an analysis of the duties imposed by law upon the local communities will show that many of what we are accustomed to conceive of as local duties are not exclusively local, but on the contrary, interest in large degree the state as a whole. The state parties, therefore, in busying themselves with local politics, have been in many instances merely discharging a function which is theirs of right. The state parties have been right in interfering with the government of local communities, further, because questions of national and state politics have in the past been more important than questions of local politics. It was right and proper, therefore, that the interests of the localities should be sacrificed to the more important interests of the state and nation.

But with the recent extraordinary development of urban life, local, and particularly municipal, questions are assuming an importance which they have never had before, and will unquestionably force themselves upon public attention. The great frequency and urgency of the cry for non-partisanship in municipal government is evidence of the fact that local questions have already forced themselves upon public notice. The national and state political parties will have to give heed to the wishes of the urban population. By the mere reason of their voting strength the people of the cities will force the parties either in their local organizations to formulate local policies, or to retire from local politics, and give place to municipal parties. Local policies will have to be considered apart from their relation to the state and nation. Opportunity will be afforded for the expression and execution by the local communities of the local will. If some amendment of the legal relation of the state to the locality is made, there is no reason to feel that in the United States the problem of the differentiation, both in its expression and in its execution, of a local from the state will cannot be solved.

The causes of the comparative failure in the United States to secure the differentiation of the local from the state will are, then, to be found in the legislative habit of enumerating in detail the powers of the local communities, in the position which the locality occupies as an agent of state government, and in the position assigned to the political party by our governmental system. This view is corroborated by English and European experience.

On the Continent, the legislature is less important, the administrative authorities are more important, than here. The legislature is more in the position of a body which vetoes, amends, or approves propositions submitted to it by the executive, than in that of a body which formulates the propositions that become law. The laws which it passes, further, deal much less with detail, much more with general principles, than do the laws passed by American legislatures. The laws applicable to the local communities naturally, therefore, do not attempt to enumerate local powers, but after granting general powers permit each locality to exercise them in such a way as to suit local conditions.   Such laws are thus general, not only in that they refer to all localities of the same class, — that is, to all cities and to all divisions similar to our counties and towns, — but also in that they confer upon such localities general and not detailed powers of local government.

This method of determining local competence of itself results in the possession by the local communities of large local powers. Such communities are not obliged to be continually asking the legislature for new powers, thus subjecting the expression of the local will to the control of the organ which expresses the will of the state as a whole. That the possession by the locality of large local powers does not result in the sacrifice of the interests of the state as a whole, is insured by the control which the state administrative authorities, in accordance with the principles of administrative centralization, have over the actions of the local communities.

Further, these local communities are not so commonly intrusted with the independent execution of general laws, as they are in this country. The political parties, which on the Continent have by no means the same strength as in this country, have neither the same opportunity nor the same temptation as here to sacrifice the interests of the local communities. They do not have the same opportunity because of the absence of special legislation and because of their own weakness. They do not have the same temptation because the efforts of parties need not, in order to bring about harmony between the state and locality, extend farther than to the election of members of the state legislature. This body controls the executive, which in its turn controls the local communities in accordance with the provisions of general law. Parties thus are not tempted to make the same use as here of the power of the legislature over the localities to promote their own interests ; nor do the political views of local administrative officers have the same importance as here. The interests of the local communities are not, therefore, so liable as in the United States to be sacrificed to those of the state as a whole.

What has been said of the Continent is true with some limitations of England. It is to be remembered that England never developed the system of local self-government to the same extent to which we have developed it in the United States. Further, almost as soon as it began to show the evil tendencies, which it would seem bound to show in the complex conditions of modern civilization, this system of local self-government was somewhat modified, and some of the principles of Continental administrative centralization were adopted. These facts have resulted in making the English legislature, from the local administrative point of view, less important than here. The centralization of the administrative system which has been going on during this century has had the effect of relieving the local communities in actual practice from the former control of Parliament, and of subjecting them to the control of the central administrative authorities.

The centralization of administration so necessary in order to secure the execution of the state will has been accompanied by a decentralization in legislation without which there can be no opportunity for the expression of a local will.

Not only does the formal governmental system as now arranged permit of the differentiation of a local will, but also the localities are relieved from the tyranny of the national parties. The national parties have no longer the same influence as formerly over the local communities, notwithstanding the fact that these parties have developed a strength in their organization which is only excelled by that of American political parties. This is so because the control over the localities has ceased to be legislative, and has become administrative. The local communities also have become less important than here as independent agents for the execution of general laws. In the discharge of the functions for which they have been formed, the state parties are, therefore, not obliged to take such a keen interest as they do in this country in local politics. The necessary harmony between the state and the locality is obtained in the governmental system, and does not have to be sought outside of it in the party. The national parties, therefore, have neither the same opportunity nor the same desire as formerly to control local politics in their own interest, and to the disadvantage of the localities themselves.

This differentiation of the local from the state will, it is to be remembered, has been brought about in Europe without the adoption of a single constitutional provision forbidding action on the part of the legislature. It has been obtained simply as the result of an enlightened public opinion, which has insisted on the establishment of proper relations between state and locality. The establishment of these relations has been obtained, it must be remembered, partly by recognizing the rights of the state, by providing for a centralization of the administrative system; partly, on the other hand, by recognizing the rights of the localities by relieving them from legislative domination, and indirectly from the despotism of the national political parties.

This happy solution of the question of the relation of state and locality has been brought about without any of those humiliating failures which are to be seen in the vain attempts of the American people to curb by constitutional limitations the power of the legislature, which seems almost universally to be regarded with distrust.

It is, of course, true that in the United States the legislative regulation of many matters has been a rank failure; but it is to be questioned whether the American legislature deserves the share of blame which is almost universally apportioned to it. It is probable that the system of government which attempts to throw the enormous burden of work upon the legislature which rests upon the American legislature, is largely to blame for present conditions. It is also probable that all attempts to curb the power of the legislature over the localities, which do not distinctly recognize that a state control must be exercised by some state authority, will fail of the success which is anticipated from them. What we need, in order to obtain harmony between the locality and the state, is to grant the locality more local legislative power than it now possesses, and to subject it to central administrative control where it is acting as the agent of the state. The way in which this can be done has been shown. It is a way upon which we have already entered, and upon which our progress would seem to be more rapid as the years roll by.

CHAPTER IV

THE FUNCTION OF ADMINISTRATION

THE function of executing the will of the state has been called administration. This function, it has been shown, must be subjected to the control of politics, if it is to be hoped that the expressed will of the state shall be executed, and thus become an actual rule of conduct. This control should not, however, extend further than is necessary to insure the execution of the state will. If it does, the spontaneous expression of the real state will tends to become difficult and the execution of that will becomes inefficient. In order to determine the exact limits to which this most necessary control should extend, it becomes necessary to analyze this function of administration.

On analysis we find that administration may be either of justice or of government. No legislature or legislative body can express the will of the state as to all matters of human conduct so clearly that no dispute as to its meaning may arise. The disputes which must necessarily arise must be set at rest before the will of the state in the concrete instances may be executed. For reasons both of convenience and of propriety, it is believed that the interpretation of the will of the state shall be made by some authority more or less independent of the legislature. The action of such non-legislative authority is usually spoken of as the administration of justice, and the authority to which this branch of the function of administration is intrusted is usually called the judicial authority.

The function of administration apart from its judicial side may be called the administration of government. The administration of government is also susceptible of differentiation. If it is analyzed it will be seen that it consists of several elements. On the border line of the administration of justice and the administration of government is a minor function of administration whose discharge is, by some governmental systems, intrusted to officers mainly busied with the administration of justice. In other systems this function is attended to by officers regarded as mainly administrative in character. To this branch of governmental activity no generic name can well be given. Its character can be made plain by concrete examples, as well as by a few words of general description.

Many laws passed by the lawgiving authority of the state are of such a character that they merely express the will of the state as a general rule of conduct. They do not, and, in the nature of things, cannot, express it in such detail that it can be executed without further governmental action, tending to bring a concrete individual or a concrete case within the class which the general rule of law purports to affect. Until the concrete case is thus brought within the general class affected by the law, the will of the state cannot be executed.

For example, the law may say that certain classes of individuals shall pay taxes on certain classes of property, and that these taxes shall vary in amount in accordance with the amount of such property. In order that the will of the state as to what tax a given individual shall pay on a given piece of property may be expressed, three things must be ascertained : viz. whether the given individual comes within the classs, whether he has property of the kind specified, and what is its amount.

Again, the law may provide that certain kinds of buildings shall be built in a specified way. In order to insure that its provisions shall be complied with, the law may provide that the plans of all buildings shall be approved by some governmental authority before their erection may be begun.

In both of these cases some action must be taken by a governmental authority, in order to bring concrete cases under the operation of general rules. So far as this is the case, the discharge of this function of government bears a close resemblance to that of the administration of justice. In some cases the matter may be attended to by authorities recognized as distinctly judicial in character, in others the fitness of distinctly judicial authorities is not so marked. Indeed, in most cases judicial authorities engaged in the decision of suits relative to merely private rights are unfitted to attend to these matters.

Judicial authorities are unfitted for the performance of these duties because such performance requires the possession of considerable technical knowledge. The proper determination of the value of property for the purpose of taxation thus requires of those who assess it considerable knowledge of property values. The approval of plans of buildings should be made by those acquainted with building processes. Therefore these matters are, as a general thing, not classed as a part of the administration of justice, but rather as a part of the administration of government.

The election of any of the officers of the government cannot, further, be had without most important action on the part of governmental

authorities. This must be as impartial and free
from prejudice as possible, if it is to be hoped
that the officers elected will represent the people
— in other words, if it is to be hoped that the
government will be popular. The action of
election officers is thus also *quasi*-judicial in
character.

In order, finally, that the general work of government may go on, the governmental organization must have at its disposal wide information
and varied knowledge. This information, which
is used not merely by the government, but as well
by private students, must in many instances be
acquired by some governmental authority which is
reasonably permanent in character. For much
of this information can be obtained only as the
result of a series of observations, lasting through
a long period of time. The authorities of the government which acquire this information must be
absolutely impartial and as free from prejudice as
possible, if it is to be hoped to get at the truth.
Their work is, therefore, quite similar to the *quasi*-
judicial work already described.

A second part of the administration of government is to be found in the mere execution of the
expressed will of the state — the law. No one
will deny that, if the expressed will of the state is
to amount to anything as an actual rule of conduct,

it must be executed. Before it can be executed it may be necessary that there shall be action taken by the judicial and *quasi*-judicial authorities to which allusion has been made. But after all this necessary action has been taken, the will of the state has to be executed. If the will of the state has been violated, the violator must be punished, and the conditions existing prior to such violation must, as far as may be, be restored.

Finally, in order that the will of the state may be either expressed or executed, a very complex governmental organization must be established, preserved, and developed. Legislators must be elected, judges must be chosen, and a whole series of officers must be provided for the discharge of the *quasi*-judicial duties already mentioned, the statistical and other similar work undertaken by the government, and for the direct execution of the will of the state. The establishment, preservation, and development of this vast force of officers and authorities should, in a popular government, be undertaken with the end in view of securing the freest possible expression by the people of the popular will, and of insuring the most efficient execution of that will after it has been expressed.[1]

[1] The duty which every state has of thus establishing, preserving, and developing its governmental organization has been called by

After this analysis of the function of administration we are in a position to answer the question put at the beginning of this chapter: What parts of this function of administration should be subjected to the control of the function of politics to the end that the expressed will of the state may be executed? It has already been shown that the administration of justice should be and is removed from this control. There remain to be considered the function of executing the law, which may be called the executive function, the *quasi*-judicial

Posada, in his valuable and suggestive *Tratado de Derecho Adminis- trativo*, the " function of administration." Posada has, however, in his analysis of governmental functions proceeded from the starting-point of motives of conduct rather than from that of functional activity. He argues that, inasmuch as it is one of the highest duties of the state to provide for itself an efficient organization, the actual pro- vision of this organization, no matter by what authority in the gov- ernment, should not be influenced by political considerations. It is of course true that the legislative and all other governmental authori- ties should determine questions of governmental organization apart from the effect which their determination may have on the fortunes of any political party. But it is also true that the formation of a par- ticular kind of governmental organization is a question of policy, and that it has frequently been the case that political parties have been organized to aid in its solution.

Posada's definition of the function of administration, while of the greatest value in emphasizing the need of recognizing that adminis- tration should not be too much subjected to the control of politics, seems also to give an inadequate idea of the extent of that function. It leaves out of consideration the vast amount of work done of a *quasi*-judicial and scientific and *quasi*-commercial character which is assuming of late such great importance.

function, the statistical and semi-scientific functions, if we may so call them, and the function of establishing, preserving, and developing the governmental organization.

As regards the executive function, as it has been called, there can be no question of the necessity of subjecting it to the control of the body intrusted ultimately with the expression of the state will. If there is no relation of subordination between the body which makes law and the body which executes it, or if, where the legislature and the executive bodies are independent of each other so far as their governmental relations are concerned, no provision is made outside of the governmental system for bringing about harmony between the making and the execution of the law, it is easy to conceive of a condition, in which the authorities provided for the execution of the law may refuse, for one reason or other, to execute it. This executive function must therefore of necessity be subordinated to the function of politics.

No such close connection, however, exists between the function of politics and the other branches of the administration of government. No control of a political character can bring it about that administrative officers will discharge better their *quasi*-judicial duties, for example, any more than such a control can bring it about that judges will make better decisions.[1]

No control which a political body can have over a body intrusted with the acquisition of facts and the gathering of information can result in the

---

[1] So far as these *quasi*-judicial functions of administrative authorities are concerned, it may be said that the Anglo-American law, as worked out in the decisions of the courts, has always regarded them as on the same footing as the well-recognized judicial functions of courts. As is said in Wilson *v.* The Mayor, 1 Denio, 595, 599, "Although the officer may not in strictness be a judge, still, if his powers are discretionary, to be exercised or withheld according to his own view of what is proper, they are judicial, and he is exempt from all responsibility by action for the motives which influence him and the manner in which such duties are performed." This rule was worked out in England at a time when, as a matter of fact, most of such duties were performed by authorities treated as parts of the judicial system, *viz.* the justices of the peace. In the United States, however, from quite an early date, such duties have been commonly discharged by authorities which were not regarded as part of the judicial system and there is a tendency somewhat to limit the rule as above laid down, so as to hold officers not holding regular courts responsible for bad faith and dishonest purposes, notwithstanding the fact of the *quasi*-judicial character of their duties. Thus in the case of Pike *v.* Megoun (44 Mo. 491) registration officers of elections were held responsible for fraudulent conduct in preventing one qualified to vote from having his name on the registration list of voters. Thus again use may be made of *mandamus* to correct arbitrary abuse of discretion by a school board, the abuse complained of consisting in selecting, for purely partisan purposes, judges and clerks from the same political party to conduct an election of members of such school board (State *v.* Board, 134 Mo. 296, 56 Amer. St. Rep. 503). This tendency is indicative of a recognition of the principle that the discharge of these *quasi*-judicial functions should be absolutely impartial and not subject to political control.

gathering of more facts or the acquisition of more exact information. The same is true, although not perhaps to the same degree, in the case of the necessary actions preliminary to the choice of officers by the electors. In these cases much must be left to official discretion, since what is demanded of the officers is not the doing of a concrete thing, but the exercise of judgment.

The courts, in the exercise of the control which the American system of government gives them over the acts of officers, have been obliged by the very force of things to recognize this distinction. Although it is possible for them to exercise a much more effective control than the legislature ever could exercise, they have voluntarily confined their jurisdiction to ministerial acts, and have refused to exercise a control over discretionary acts. The only possible exception to this statement is to be found in the fact that the courts will see to it that discretion is not grossly abused. This is the only point over which the legislature, or similar political body, can exercise a control over the discharge of this branch of administration. All that the legislature, or any political body, can do is to see to it, through the exercise of its control, that persons discharging these administrative functions are efficient and impartial. Their general conduct, but not their concrete actions, should be subject to control.

It is not only true that the control which the political body should and may have over the executive authority cannot, in the nature of things, be exercised over an administrative authority, *i.e.* an authority discharging that part of the function of administration not distinctly of an executive character; but any attempt to exercise such a control beyond the attempt to insure administrative integrity is likely to produce evil rather than good. For a close connection between politics and work of an administrative character is liable, in the case of the work done by the administration in the investigation of facts and the gathering of information, to pollute the sources of truth, in that it may give a bias to the investigator. It is liable in the case of an officer intrusted with the discharge of the *quasi*-judicial duties to produce corruption, in that it may take from him that impartiality which is so necessary. The same reasons which demand an impartial and upright administration of justice call for an impartial and upright administration of these matters of government. Private right may be as easily violated by a corrupt and partial administration of a tax law as by a corrupt and partial judicial decision. Political rights are easily violated by corrupt and partial election officers. Political control over administrative functions is liable finally to produce inefficient administration in that it makes administrative officers feel that what is demanded of them is not so much work that will improve their own department, as compliance with the behests of the political party.

Up to within comparatively few years, the existence of this branch of the administration of government has been practically ignored. Officers whose main duty was the execution of the law in the sense in which these words have been used in these pages have attended to these administrative matters. The distinctly administrative functions naturally were confused with the executive function. It was regarded as proper to attempt to exercise the same control over administrative matters as was exercised, and properly exercised, over the executive function. When, however, administrative matters began to assume greater prominence with the extension of the field of government, — an extension which was largely made in regard to subjects of an administrative rather than of an executive character, — the evil effects of such a treatment of matters of administration could not fail to appear. It is only in those countries which have recognized most fully that administration apart from its executive side is not from the point of view of theory, and should not be from the point of view of fact, connected with politics, that the greatest progress has been made in the improvement of the details of government, which, as in every other field of life, count for so much, — much more, in fact, than the general principles.

The necessity for this separation of politics from administration is very marked in the case of municipal government. For municipal government is very largely a matter of administration in the narrow sense of the word. This is the truth at the bottom of the claim which is so often made, that municipal government is a matter of business. Of course the statement of the truth in this form is not correct. For municipal government is not business, but government. It is, however, almost exclusively a matter of administration, and a matter of local administration.

While it is true that politics should have no more to do with state than with municipal administration, using the word in the narrow sense, it is also true that the influence of politics on municipal government is worse than on state administration. This is so, because municipal government is in character more administrative than state government, and because, when politics affect municipal government it is liable to be not only local, but also state and national, politics. The result is, not only that municipal government is rendered partial, unjust, and inefficient, but that municipal interests are sacrificed to national and state interests. Those countries like England and Germany, whose public opinion has most clearly distinguished administration from politics, and state from local politics, will be found to have been most successful in their solution of the problem of municipal government.

The fact is, then, that there is a large part of administration which is unconnected with politics, which should therefore be relieved very largely, if not altogether, from the control of political bodies. It is unconnected with politics because it embraces fields of semi-scientific, *quasi*-judicial and *quasi*-business or commercial activity — work which has little if any influence on the expression of the true state will. For the most advantageous discharge of this branch of the function of administration there should be organized a force of governmental agents absolutely free from the influence of politics. Such a force should be free from the influence of politics because of the fact that their mission is the exercise of foresight and discretion, the pursuit of truth, the gathering of information, the maintenance of a strictly impartial attitude toward the individuals with whom they have dealings, and the provision of the most efficient possible administrative organization. The position assigned to such officers should be much the same as is that which has been by universal consent assigned to judges. Their work is no more political in character than is that of judges; and while it may be that their organization should differ somewhat from the judicial organization, still, the most advantageous discharge of the work devolved upon them makes it necessary that their position should be much the same as that which we assign to judicial officers.

It took the world a long time to recognize that judicial officers should occupy the position they now hold. In England, this position was not assigned to them by law until the passage of the Act of Settlement in 1701. In some of the Continental European countries such a position cannot even now be regarded as theirs.[1] Before this position could be thus assigned to judges, the existence of the judicial function as a function not connected with politics had to be recognized. So, before we can hope that administrative officers can occupy a position reasonably permanent in character and reasonably free from political influence, we must recognize the existence of an administrative function whose discharge must be uninfluenced by political considerations. This England and Germany, and France though to a

[1] For example, France and Italy; see Lowell, *Government and Parties in Continental Europe*, Vol. I., pp. 51, 176.

much less degree, have done. To this fact in large part is due the excellence of their administrative systems. Under such conditions the government may safely be intrusted with much work which, until the people of the United States attain to the same conception, cannot be intrusted to their governmental organs. For when so undertaken by governmental organs, it is inefficiently done, and inefficiently done because of our failure to recognize the existence of an administrative function which should be discharged by authorities not subject to the influence of politics.

The governmental authorities intrusted with the discharge of the administrative function should not only, like judges, be free from the influence of politics; they should also, again like judges, have considerable permanence of tenure. They should have permanence of tenure because the excellence of their work is often conditioned by the fact that they are expert, and expertness comes largely from long practice. Reasonable permanence of tenure is absolutely necessary for the semi-scientific, *quasi*-judicial, and technical branches of the administrative service. It is also extremely desirable for a much larger part of the administrative service, whose duties are not so important to the welfare of the state as those of the semi-scientific, *quasi*-judicial, and technical branches just mentioned. This is that vast class of clerical and ministerial officers who simply carry out orders of superiors in whose hands is the determination of general questions of administrative policy.　Reasonable permanence of tenure is desirable for this class of officers because without it the maximum of administrative efficiency is impossible of attainment.　Without it, it is true, the work of government can go on, but without it the cost of government is vastly increased, while the work is poorly done.　Such permanence of tenure can be secured by provision of law, as is the case in Germany, or it may be secured by the demands of an enlightened public opinion, as is the case in England.

Care should be taken, however, that permanence of tenure be not given to those distinctly executive officers to whom is entrusted the general execution of the law.　If permanence of tenure is provided for such officers, the government, as a whole, will tend to lose its popular character, since the execution of law has an important influence on the expression of the will of the state.　An unenforced law is not really a rule of conduct, and the enforcement of law is in the hands of such officers.　If, therefore, officers intrusted with the execution of the law are not subjected to some control of a political character provided in the governmental organization, as, for example, the control of the legislature, they should be subject to the control of the party which, in such case, is called upon to exercise that political control over the general function of administration so indispensable to a harmonious and efficient government.

Switzerland is practically the only country possessing a popular government where the highest executive officials are not recognized as political in the sense that they change with a change in the popular will. This anomalous condition of affairs is probably due, in large part, to the frank recognition that these officers are mere ministerial agents of the legislature, — the political body in the government *par excellence*, — and to the unquestioned existence of the power of the legislature to remove them from office at any time. As Mr. Lowell says: "The relation of the executive to the legislature in Switzerland differs from that of every other nation. The Federal Council is not, like the President of the United States, a separate branch of the government, which has a power of final decision within its own sphere of action. It has been given no veto upon laws to prevent encroachment upon its rights, and even in executive matters it has, strictly speaking, no independent authority at all, for it seems that its administrative acts can be supervised, controlled, or reversed by the Federal Assembly. . . . If the

Assembly disagrees with them [the Councillors] in legislative or executive matters, they submit to its will as the final authority, and try loyally to carry out its directions." [1]   Again Mr. Lowell says : " The Federal Council is essentially a business body, and in selecting candidates more attention is paid to executive capacity than to political leadership.   Its duty consists in conducting the administration and giving advice on legislation. But it is not expected to control the policy of the state, and herein lies the real secret of its position." [2]

Permanence of tenure in the case of the highest executive officers entrusted with large discretionary powers is incompatible with popular government, since it tends to further the formation of an immense governmental machine whose very efficiency may make it dangerous to the existence of popular government.   It is to be remembered that too great strength in the administrative organization tends to make popular government impossible.   Thus a strong administration, where the party organization is weak, may nullify the popular will through the control which the administration has, and in the nature of things must

[1] *Government and Parties in Continental Europe*, Vol. II., p. 197 *et seq.*
[2] *Ibid.*, p. 200.

have, over the elections. This is largely true at
the present time of Germany, and has been true
in the past in France. On the other hand, it is
to be remembered that an administrative system,
where permanence of tenure in the lower grades
of the service does not exist at all, can also be
made use of, where there is a strong party organization, to nullify the popular will. This may be
done through the wrongful exercise of the power
of appointment, under a party system so formed
as to make the popular will in the party difficult
of expression.

In the semi-scientific, *quasi*-judicial, clerical, and
ministerial divisions of the administrative system
provision should be made for permanence of tenure, if efficient and impartial administration is to
be expected, and if questions of policy are to be
determined in accordance with the popular will.
In its higher divisions, that is, those where the
incumbents of offices have a determining influence
on questions of policy, and particularly in case of
the executive head, permanence of tenure should
be avoided. Provision should in these cases be
made for political control if it is hoped to secure
the decision of questions of policy by bodies representative of the people.

Enough has been said, it is hoped, to show that
while two primary functions of government may

be differentiated, the questions arising out of the discharge of the one cannot, in a popular government, be considered apart from the questions arising out of the discharge of the other. In order that the execution of the will of the state shall conform to its expression, that is, in order that the functions of politics and administration may be co-ordinated, the political body in the governmental system must have control over the administrative body. There are limits, however, beyond which such a control should not be exercised. If it is extended to all officers in the administrative service, the government becomes inefficient and incapable of attending to many matters which for their advantageous attention must be attended to by the government. The too great extension of the political control, where the party organization has great strength and the administrative system is weak, tends further to defeat the very purpose for which it is formed. For the administrative organization may be made use of to further the ends of the party and to prevent the free expression of the state will.

On the other hand, if the attempt is made to strengthen the administrative system unduly in the hope of securing efficient administration, there is danger that, if the party organization is weak, the administrative organization may be made use of to influence the expression of the will of the state through its power over elections. Safety lies alone in frankly recognizing both that there should be a control over the general execution of the law and that there is a part of the work of administration into which politics should not enter. Only in this way may really popular government and efficient administration be obtained.

CHAPTER V

THE EFFECT OF THE ADMINISTRATIVE SYSTEM ON THE RELATIONS OF POLITICS AND ADMINISTRATION

THE administrative systems of the world belong in a greater or less degree to one of two main forms. Either officers who have in their hands the execution of the will of the state are vested with large discretion, so much in fact as to make them really organs for the expression of the will of the state in its minor details; or they are vested with almost no discretion at all, being merely the instruments of other state organs which determine, not only what shall be done, but also how the thing determined upon shall be done. The first system of administration bears upon it the impress of the time when there was in the organization of government no clear distinction between the functions of politics and administration, and when little or no attempt was made to obtain the expression of the popular will. The second evidences the extreme to which popular government has gone in the attempt to make the popular will felt in all the details of the government.

The first system of administration is, as a general thing, characterized by a hierarchy of officers, in which the subordinates owe allegiance to the superior officers rather than to the law of the land, and in which superior officers have a right of direction, control, and supervision over a host of subordinates. If the general system of government has become popular in character, such superiors are subjected to a control more or less effective, in accordance with the degree in which the government is popular in character, exercised by the body which has obtained the right ultimately to express the popular will.

The second system of administration recognizes little if any relation of subordination of one officer to another, but lays emphasis on the allegiance of each to the law as laid down by the body having the right to express the will of the state.[1] Each official is equal to any other before the law; to it alone he is subordinated, and to it alone he is to look for directions. Of course no concrete government ever was or could be based on exactly such principles as have just been outlined. Anarchy would be the result of any such attempt. For the

[1] Cf. Freund, " American Administrative Law," *Political Science Quarterly*, Vol. IX., p. 403.

legislature was never organized which could exercise over such a governmental system the control necessary to insure the carrying out of its will. Responsibility is too diffused to be effective.

At the same time the legislature may rely on officers, intrusted with the administration of justice rather than with the administration of government, to exercise the necessary control over those officers who are to execute its will. This control may be exercised either on the application of individuals whose rights have been violated, or on that of administrative officials who have, to this extent, been given supervisory powers. The necessary central control may thus be vested in the judicial authorities, as the authorities charged with the interpretation of the law. That is, while important administrative officers may be subjected to the control of the courts in their execution of the law, they may be relieved almost entirely from the control and supervision of any administrative superior, and may be subject to legislative control only to the extent that the legislature may regulate their powers and duties in great detail. They owe allegiance to the law contained in this detailed legislation, which they may be forced by the courts to observe.

This system of administration is usually accompanied by extreme decentralization from the point of view of the relations of the state to the local communities. It has been termed "a government of laws, and not of men." It has unquestioned advantages, particularly in retarding the development of despotism and in preventing arbitrary administrative action; but it makes the development of the administrative function free from the influences of politics almost impossible, since it tends to promote interference by the legislature, a distinctly political body, in all matters of government. The judicial control by which it is accompanied is not suited to secure anything except obedience to the law. It can hardly be used at all from the point of view of expediency. These questions of expediency must be determined by the legislature, which must descend in its legislation into the greatest details.

Such a system of administration tends not only to promote legislative interference, but also to make permanence of tenure impossible for officers whose duty is to execute the law. For detailed legislation and judicial control over its execution are not sufficient to produce harmony between the governmental body which expresses the will of the state, and the governmental authority which executes that will. The same body which makes the rule of law has the right neither to execute it nor to control the execution of it. The executive officers may or may not enforce the law as it was intended by the legislature. Judicial officers, in exercising control over such executive officers, may or may not take the same view of the law as did the legislature. No provision is thus made in the governmental organization for securing harmony between the expression and execution of the will of the state. The people, the ultimate sovereign in a popular government, must, however, have a control over the officers who execute their will, as well as over those who express it. Such executive officers are therefore given short terms, are thus subject to a popular control which may be frequently exercised because of frequent elections.[1]

The system of administration which has just been described was the system which was either adopted by the states of the American Union at the time of their formation or was soon after developed. It was a logical development of that brought here from England. The course of political development in England at the time this country was colonized resulted in giving Parliament the dominant position in the government.

[1] So far as the will of the state is expressed by the central legislature and executed by officers locally elected, this popular control does not by any means insure harmony between the expression and execution of the will of the state, since the will of the locality which executes the law may not be in accord with the will of the state which is expressed in the law.

Inasmuch as there was no written constitution for the English government, there were no formal limitations on the power of Parliament. It is true, Parliament had not, at the time when the American system of government was framed, claimed the powers that it later exercised. But in the constitutional struggles that had been going on in England the legislature, that is, Parliament, was regarded by that class of people from which the American colonies had been in large part recruited as their bulwark against despotism, and the legal recognition of its theoretically supreme position in the new American governments was naturally considered as both proper and desirable. This supremacy of the legislature was in England combined, particularly so far as the relations of local officers to the central government was concerned, with great practical administrative independence. Local administrative officers owed allegiance to the law of the land, *i.e.* the statutes of Parliament, rather than to a central administrative superior; and their obedience to that law was secured by their subjection to the control of the courts.

This administrative independence of local officers had been of the greatest service in preventing the Stuarts from imposing upon England the despotic régime of government for whose sake the

Stuart dynasty finally sacrificed itself. Indeed it was largely due to this administrative system that Parliament was successful in its struggles with the Crown. It was only natural, therefore, that the administrative system which in these struggles had been tried and not found wanting should be adopted in the new state governments established in America at the end of the eighteenth century.

But the system of administration originally established in this country, while based on that of England, differed from the English system in several respects. The English system still had many characteristics which recalled the time when the powers of the Crown were greater than those of Parliament, and when the complete administrative independence of administrative officers had not developed. Thus, both at the centre and in the localities, administrative officers were formally appointed by the Crown. These characteristics were, however, abandoned by the framers of the new governments on this side of the Atlantic. They made a complete break with the formal institutions of the past, and based their new governments on the principle of popular control.

This principle it was whose adoption necessitated the adoption of the principle of elective officers and frequent elections. Provision was made, therefore, ultimately for electing all important

officers of government and for giving them short
terms of office. At first it was the legislature
which elected the main officers of the central
government of the state, while the people had
the power of electing their local representatives.
Later on the principle of popular election was
applied to all officers indiscriminately, until it may
be said that by the middle of this century practically all state officers of any importance, whether
central or local (including in the latter term municipal officers), were elected by the people either of
the state as a whole or of the locality in which such
officers had jurisdiction, and served for short terms.

The result was to make impossible any state
administrative supervision over the main body of
officers intrusted with the execution of the law.
All the control which could be exercised in the
governmental system in the interest of producing
coördination between the functions of expressing
and executing the will of the state had to be
found in the power of the legislature to regulate
in detail the duties of officers intrusted with the
execution of the law. The courts had to be
trusted, on the application, either of individuals
whose rights were violated, or of officers who by
express terms of statute were given power to make
such applications themselves, to force obedience
to this detailed legislation.

The control to be found in this power of detailed legislation, it is to be noted, was exercised by a body which was confessedly political in character, a body, further, which was in the nature of things not possessed of large administrative knowledge, and whose main purpose was to express the will of the people by whom it was elected. But notwithstanding the political character of the legislature and its theoretically limitless powers of control, its organization was of such a character, and necessarily of such a character, that the exercise of its control in concrete cases was impracticable.

The very general adoption of the principle of the separation of powers in the American constitutions made it impossible for the legislature to exercise any important power of control over executive officers through the exercise of any power of removal. All the legislature could do, if it were dissatisfied with the way in which officers acted who were intrusted with the execution of the law, was to regulate their duties more in detail, trusting to the courts to enforce its mandates. The control of the courts was almost as unsatisfactory as that of the legislature. They could take action only in cases of glaring disobedience, and were hampered in their exercise of even this power by the existence of juries which reflected in their verdicts the popular feelings of the localities from which they were selected.

Probably the most marked instance of the failure of this legislative control over officers intrusted with the execution of the law, offered by this system of administration, is to be found in the case of the prohibition or excise laws passed during the first half of this century. The people of several of the states became so convinced of the evils of intemperance that they either resorted to the expedient of absolutely prohibiting the sale of liquor as a beverage, or adopted very stringent laws which were intended to diminish its use. This was the expression of the will of the state as to this subject. When, however, it came to execute this will, it was found that the system of administration provided no means of coördinating the execution with the expression of the will of the state. The laws passed by the legislatures immediately afterwards descended successively into greater and greater detail, in the hope that in this way the execution of the will of the state might be secured.[1] In some states the attempt was made to take away the powers of the jury as to this matter by providing that in case of the illegal sale of liquor, injunction should issue to

[1] Sites, "Centralized Administration of Liquor Laws in the American Commonwealths," *Col. Univ. Pub.*, Vol. X., No. 3.

restrain its sale, and that violations of the law after the issue of the injunction should be punished as contempt of court.   Such is said to be the origin of "government by injunction." [1]

In the case of these prohibition and excise laws it is of course true that the will of the state as expressed by the legislature was not the will of many of the localities, which controlling, through the system of local elections, the execution of that will, were able as a matter of fact to nullify it, so far as concerned its force as an actual rule of conduct for the citizens of the particular locality.   But even where there was no such conflict between the state and the locality, there was no method of coördinating the execution with the expression of the state will.   The officers intrusted with the execution of the state will were not subjected to the control of a central administrative authority, which in its turn was subjected to an effective control to be exercised by the legislature.   These officers might or they might not, as they saw fit, execute the will of the state.   Every executive officer, although, by the theory of the system, intrusted merely with the execution of the law, became in a measure, and in a large measure, a political officer.

Now, if the government was to go on harmoni-

[1] See Dunbar, "Government by Injunction," in *Law Quarterly Review*, December, 1897.

ously, some means of coördinating the expression
and execution of the will of the state had to be
found. Such means could not be found in the
governmental system, as has been shown. It had
therefore to be found outside of the government in
some extra-legal institution. It was, as a matter of
fact, found in the political party. The party took
upon itself the burden of selecting, not merely
the members of the body which, by the theory of
the governmental system, expressed the will of the
state, *i.e.* the legislature, but also those persons
who were to execute that will, *i.e.* the executive
officers. The party had to choose the central
executive officers because the adoption of the
principle of the separation of powers had relieved
them from any effective legislative control. The
party had to choose all local officers because the
extremely decentralized character of the administrative system relieved them from any effective
state control. To do this work the party organization had to be both strong and permanent.

The party organization had to be strong because,
in order to afford any guarantee that the will of
the people should actually be executed, all elected
officers had to be pledged individually to follow a
certain line of conduct, and the party had to
assume responsibility for them, and had to formulate in advance what came to be called a platform.

Upon this platform each candidate was supposed to stand, and its formal acceptance was demanded of each candidate for an important office. The individual candidate was thus necessarily sunk in the party. It was largely for this reason that the individual professions of faith which under other governmental systems are often made by each candidate are practically unknown to American public life.

It is mainly because of the absolute necessity for the coördination of the functions of politics and administration, a coördination which, as has been shown, could not be obtained in the governmental system, and must be found in the party organization, that party regularity, as it is called, has been so prized in the United States. If it had not been for this strong allegiance to party, which is almost peculiar to American politics, our government would have consisted of a disorderly, uncoördinated, unregulated crowd of officers, each equal in actual power and authority to every other, and each acting according to the dictates of his own conscience or the caprice of his own individual whims, though all were supposedly engaged merely in the execution of laws, as detailed as could well be imagined, and formulating the supposed will of the people represented in the legislature.

This strong party organization further was made

necessary in the state and in the more complex
local governments, viz. the cities, by the mere
number of officers to be elected. The feeling of
neighborhood, which results in large knowledge
on the part of the electors of the merits of the
various candidates for public office, and which
exercises such an influence for good in the rural
districts, cannot be expected in the nature of things
to play much of a rôle either in the state as a
whole, or in the cities, where the people know little
of each other. The voters must rely, in their
choice of state and city officers, where many are
chosen, upon the party whose platform appeals to
them and whose past record is such that they can
trust its promises as to future conduct. Attempts
to act outside of party, while unquestionably of
great educational value in many instances, will
in such conditions most frequently have no immediate results of a practical value on existing
political issues.

The party organization which took upon itself
the burden of coördinating the functions of expressing and executing the will of the state in
the American governmental system, had to be not
merely strong but also permanent. It had to be
permanent, if for no other reason, because no one
election ordinarily resulted in producing harmonious relations between the policy-determining, that

is, the political, body in the government, and the policy-executing, or administrative, body. This was so because it was, and for that matter, it is, seldom that at one election all the elective officers whose duty it is to execute the laws are elected. The terms of such officers are not as a general thing coincident. The work of the party is therefore not done at one election. It must keep up its organization, prepared to battle for the issues which it desires to further, on the occasion of every one of the numerous elections made necessary by the administrative system. Otherwise it will not have discharged this function of coördinating the expression and the execution of the will of the state which is demanded of it, and which can be obtained alone through it.

The task of keeping together a party having so much work to do, is not, however, an easy one. Those persons who interest themselves in the work of party management and of carrying on the government, cannot be expected to devote the time and energy necessary to this work, which is enormous, from purely disinterested motives. As Bryce observes: "To rely on public duty as the main motive power in politics is to assume a commonwealth of angels. Men such as we know them must have some other inducement."[1] They must

[1] *American Commonwealth*, 3d edition, Vol. II., p. 59.

be paid in some way. Indeed the work is so ardu-
ous as to take all of their time. They cannot live,
therefore, if they are not endowed with this world's
goods, unless pecuniary rewards are attached to
the pursuit of party politics. If such rewards are
not attached by law to this work, ways will and
must be found outside of the law by which they
will be provided. As a matter of fact, ways have
been provided by law in many cases. That is, the
American law as a general thing attaches a salary,
in some instances considerable in amount, to most
offices, both legislative and executive. The necessity of keeping up the party organization makes it
seem necessary to regard these salaried offices as
rewards for party service.

We may conclude from what has been said, that
the extremely loose and unconcentrated administrative system obtaining in this country, has made
impossible the coördination in the governmental
system of the functions of expressing and executing the will of the state, that as a result, the officers intrusted with the execution of the law, *i.e.*
the will of the state, have become really political
in character, since upon their decision has rested
very largely the determination whether a rule
of law as laid down in a legislative statute shall
become an actually enforced rule of conduct. To
obtain the necessary coördination between these

two functions, the political party, an extra-governmental institution, has been appealed to The party organization has had to be made very strong and comparatively permanent in order to do the work demanded; and the keeping of it together has made it seem necessary to regard party service as a justifiable ground for obtaining the rewards to be found in the offices.

Under such a system, which is based on a large number of elective offices, permanence in office has been the exception rather than the rule. The people have regarded the frequent changes in the official force as not only unavoidable but as proper. They have seen that a system of administration, which makes even unimportant elective officers political in character, in that they have in their hands the uncontrolled execution of the law, must submit to frequent changes in its official force.

Some of the extreme advocates of this system have referred to it as a distinctly American system. They have even gone further and claimed that when adopted, not merely in the case of elective officers, but also in the case of appointive officers occupying positions where the opportunity to exercise discretion is very slight if it exists at all, the system can be justified on the same grounds. That the American system of government, as this system has been called and properly called, has,

in its later development, applied the same rules
to those ministerial appointive officers cannot be
denied. That the real principle underlying this
system necessitates such action must, however, be
denied. The reason why such ministerial appointive officers have been treated in the same way as
discretionary elected officers, is to be found in the
desire to keep up the party organization and to
maintain its strength. The necessity of keeping
up the party organization was deemed so great
that the theory that offices should be regarded as
spoils with which the victorious party was to be
rewarded, was adopted.

The adoption of the "spoils system," as it was
called, was possible because of the failure to distinguish administration from politics, promoted by
the character of the administrative system. See-
ing a great body of elected officials changed frequently, the people naturally did not protest when
the principle of "rotation in office," as it was
called, was applied as well to appointed ministerial officers." It is true, of course, that certain of
the most prominent statesmen of the time called
attention to the evils which would result from the
adoption of the principle of rotation in office of
these appointed officers.[1] But it is to be remem-

[1] See Fifteenth Report of the United States Civil Service Commission, Part VI., p. 443, which contains an excellent history of the
development of the spoils system. See also Ford, *op. cit.*, Chap. XI.

bered that at the time the spoils system got its hold on American public life, the distinctly administrative functions were not so important as they later became. This was due to the fact that, our civilization being comparatively simple, the work of the government was not nearly so extensive or complicated as it is now.

The spoils system was first introduced in the state of New York, whose politics, even in colonial times, were probably more bitter than elsewhere. It was taken from New York into the national administration at about the time when, owing to the democratic movement beginning with 1820, and the slavery question, the political struggles of the nation began to assume somewhat the same bitterness which had characterized the politics of New York. Thence it spread through the entire Union, and soon began to be regarded as an essential part of the American political system.

The spoils system, considered from the point of view of political theory, consisted in subjecting all officers, discretionary or ministerial, appointive or elective, who were intrusted with the execution of the law, to the control of the political party, the body which in the American political system had the task of coördinating the functions of politics and administration.

The spoils system had, however, two great faults.

In the first place, when applied to ministerial appointive officers, it seriously impaired administrative efficiency. In the second place, even where applied to elective officers, and much more so when applied to appointive officers, where it had no theoretical justification except that to be found in the necessity of keeping up the party organization, it tended to aid in the formation of political party machines, organized not so much for facilitating the expression of the will of the state as for keeping the party in power. It thus aided in making the party an end rather than a means. The party, largely owing to the spoils system, gradually ceased to discharge, as fully as it should, the function of facilitating the expression of the will of the state, and indeed in many instances came to be a hindrance rather than an aid.

The evil of decreased administrative efficiency first became noticeable. It naturally attracted attention in the national administration sooner than in that of the states. This was so because the formal administrative system of the national government did not lend itself so readily as did the state administrative system to the idea which it has been pointed out was at the bottom of the spoils system. The national administrative system differed at the time of its formation considerably from that obtaining in the states. It embodied, much more than did that of the states, the principles of the English system which have promoted the development in England during the present century of considerable centralization in administration. Thus the principle of popular election, which, even at the time the national government was formed, had begun to win popular approval in the states, received no recognition in the national Constitution. Practically all national officers were, by the Constitution, to be appointed by the chief executive or by his appointees.

The national administrative system had in it, from the beginning, the germs of administrative centralization. So far as this was the case it was somewhat reactionary from the point of view of the American political development of that time. These germs of administrative centralization could not fail in a favorable environment to develop into a centralized administrative system. The favorable environment was found, in the first place, in the rigidity of the national Constitution. This rigidity did not permit of easy amendment, and, therefore, prevented the development in the national government of the decentralized unconcentrated administrative system which was characteristic of the state governments of the latter part of the first half of this century. This favorable environment was found, in the second place, in the latent powers vested in the President, whose recognition has resulted in subjecting the entire national administrative system to his control.

In 1789 the Senate of the United States determined that the power of removal was vested in the President alone. Although from 1867 to 1887 Congress receded from this position by the passage of the Tenure of Office Acts, the exercise of the power of removal by the President, uncontrolled by any other governmental authority for the seventy-five years succeeding the formation of our national administrative system, had resulted not only in giving the President the power of directing the entire national administration, but also in obtaining universal acknowledgment that the President was the head of the administrative system of the national government. For his directions were sanctioned at first in actual practice and later in constitutional theory by the threat of removal. The question was settled practically when Jackson removed his Secretary of the Treasury for not obeying his directions relative to withdrawing the United States funds on deposit in the United States Bank. Jackson's action was not followed by any serious and permanent protest on the part of the other organs of the United States government, and met with the unquestioned approval of the great mass of the people. By the repeal of the Tenure of Office Acts in 1887, the national government was again definitely committed to the policy of centralized administration. This power of removal has recently been recognized by the United States Supreme Court.[1]

While, then, the states were developing a very decentralized administrative system, the United States was developing a very centralized system. Space does not permit any detailed account of this development. It must suffice to call attention to the national financial administration, and to several decisions of the Supreme Court applicable in principle to all administrative services. Originally the method of administering the national finances was very similar to that in vogue in the states. That is, in each of the administrative districts provided for the purpose was placed an officer called the collector of customs, who had to interpret the law to the best of his judgment, and who was not subject to the instructions of the Secretary of the Treasury, the nominal head of the system.[2] Such a system, however, naturally resulted in lack of administrative uniformity at the different ports of the United States, and gradually the law recognized more and more the supervisory

[1] Parsons *v.* United States, 167 U. S. 324.

[2] See Report of the Secretary of the Treasury on the Collection of Duties, 1885, p. xxxvi.

and directing power of the Secretary of the Treasury, who was aided in his work by a corps of special agents. The main duty of these officers is to visit the various customs districts and bring about harmony in the actions of the various collectors. For quite a time, further, the law made express provision for an appeal to the Secretary of the Treasury from the decisions of the customs collectors. The same principle was, and is now, applied to the administration of the internal revenue.

The result of this development has been the recognition of an official hierarchy in the national administration, with the power in the heads of departments to reverse or modify, on appeal of persons interested, the decisions of the inferior officers, and to direct the actions of these officers. The United States Supreme Court has recognized the right of the courts by *mandamus* to force an inferior officer to carry out the decisions of his superior,[1] and the right of an individual deeming himself aggrieved by the decisions of an inferior to appeal to a superior.[2]

[1] United States *v.* Black, 128 U. S. 540 ; United States *v.* Raum, 135 U. S. 200.

[2] See Butterworth *v.* United States, 112 U. S. 50 ; see also United States *v.* Cobb, 11 Federal Reporter, 76, which also recognizes the right of the head of a United States Executive Department to change the decision of a subordinate.

At the head of this official hierarchy stands the President, with large if not complete powers of appointment, removal, direction, and supervision. This conception of the centralized character of the national administration system may be said to have been reached by about the middle of the century, and is expressed in an opinion of the Attorney-General of the United States, where it is said: " I hold that no head of a department can lawfully perform an official act against the will of the President; and that will is by the Constitution to govern the performance of all such acts." [1]

This centralization of the national administration prevented subordinate officers from becoming political in character, in that it deprived them of discretionary powers and subjected their actions to the control of a superior. It was not necessary, therefore, to subject them to the control of the political party in order to bring about that coördination between the functions of politics and administration which has been shown to be so important. The control of the party over the President and heads of departments was sufficient. This control the parties have had almost from the beginning of the national government. It is now universally recognized that the heads of all executive depart-

[1] 7 Opinions of the Attorneys-General, 453, 470 ; see also Goodnow, *Comparative Administrative Law,* I., p. 66, *et seq.*

ments shall belong to the same political party which has elected the President.

The enormous increase in the administrative work of the national government, much of which was of a semi-scientific character, — *e.g.* the patent office administration, the geological survey, the work of various statistical bureaus, — made the loss of administrative efficiency, due to the adoption of the spoils idea, very prominent. The demand was made as early as 1841 that some means should be adopted which should make the administration more efficient. A committee of the House of Representatives appointed in that year, reported that "the habit of applying mere political tests to the mass of appointments is believed to be injurious to the public service, by often filling important offices with incompetent men," and proposed the adoption of preliminary examinations for those desiring to enter the civil service.[1] In 1853, pass examinations were provided, in the hope that absolute incompetence might be denied entrance into the civil service.[2] This method was not effective, and in 1872, in imitation of English precedents adopted to remedy evils similar to those which had appeared here, open competitive examinations

[1] Fifteenth Report, United States Civil Service Commission, p. 466.
[2] *Ibid.*, p. 474.

were introduced.[1]   Since 1883, when the present
civil service law was passed, these examinations
have been steadily made necessary for more and
more ministerial appointive positions whose incumbents could not exercise an appreciable influence
on the general policy of the government, until
now nearly eighty-seven thousand positions are
subject to the Civil Service Rules.[2]

The last step that has been taken is the attempt
to prevent removals for political reasons.   The
recent order of the President[3] on this subject thus
recognizes that a vast body of ministerial administrative officers shall be taken out of the control of
the parties.[4]

Open competitive examinations for entrance into
the civil service, although they embody in the
minds of most people all the purposes of civil
service reform, are really but a small part of this
reform.   Its ultimate object is the recognition of
a function of government whose discharge, like
that of the administration of justice, shall be free
from the influences of politics.   This ultimate
object is made evident in the recent order of the

[1] See United States Revised Statutes, § 1753.

[2] Fifteenth Report, United States Civil Service Commission,
p. 141.

[3] Civil Service Rule II., Sect. 8.

[4] It has been held by the Supreme Court that this order cannot
be enforced by injunction.   White *v.* Berry, 171 U. S. 366.

President relative to removals. Competitive examinations can, in the nature of things, be applied successfully only to comparatively unimportant positions in the service. They will, however, have amply justified their adoption if, in addition to relieving the lower branches of the service from the influence of politics, they succeed in impressing on the public mind the feeling that it is not necessary either in the national government, nor, for that matter, in many cases in the present state governments, to accord the political parties the great powers they have possessed in the past over governmental officers whose only duty is to aid in the execution of the laws. Once that idea is possessed by the public, it will be a comparatively easy matter to insist that officers of greater importance, such as chiefs of divisions, collectors of customs and internal revenue, postmasters, even, in many cases, commissioners of bureaus, shall be selected on account of fitness for their positions, and shall, so long as they give evidence of such fitness, be retained in office. That this can be accomplished by any changes in the law may, perhaps, be doubted. That it will be accomplished, as soon as an educated and intelligent public opinion demands it, is a moral certainty.

Not only does the history of England, where the movement has progressed further than in this country, prove this forecast to be correct, its correctness may also be inferred from the most recent development in the states of the United States which have attained the most complex civilization. The American system of administration as seen in the state governments reached its apogee about the middle of this century.   That is, by that time, the elective principle with all its resulting incidents had been pretty generally adopted.   By that time, however, the course of administrative decentralization had been run, and the tendency since that time has been to centralize the state administration in somewhat the same way as the national administration has been centralized.   This change in public feeling has been due partly to the great increase in the work of the state governments, which has been particularly characteristic of the last quarter of the nineteenth century, and to the tremendous development of urban life with which every one is familiar.   It has been due also, in part, to the change in our social and economic conditions brought about by the application of steam and electricity.   An administrative system suited for sparsely populated localities bound together by the stage-coach and the mail-carrier, was unsuited for densely populated districts united by the railroad, the telegraph, and the telephone. What had before been separated were united.

The administrative system had to be centralized to suit changed conditions.

The state government has within comparatively recent times assumed the supervision of many matters like banking, insurance, agricultural products, manufactures, and industrial life generally, and transportation, which not so long ago were not objects of governmental activity. The growth of large cities has forced on public attention problems which in rural conditions could be left to private individuals to solve. The treatment of all these subjects has involved a great increase in the extent of the administrative function as it has been described. The traditional American system of administration, which hardly recognized that there was an administrative function at all, broke down when confronted with these problems, in the same way that a similar system, which existed in England at the beginning of this century, had previously broken down.

The problems of modern civilization came to the front first in the cities, and made necessary a vast increase in the administrative functions of municipal government. The loss of efficiency occasioned by the old methods was most marked, and made changes therein extremely desirable. The first attempt made to apply the necessary remedies was to concentrate and centralize the municipal administration. This is seen in the almost universal movement toward according the mayor the same position in the city that the President has come to occupy in the nation. Progress has, however, been more difficult in the case of the mayor than in that of the President. This is so, because the traditions which existed in the case of the city, did not exist in the case of the national government. The President obtained the position which he occupies, as the head of the national administrative system, without many important changes in the law, but as the result of natural evolution. The mayor's position, however, could not be changed without changes in the law, which in their turn could be made only by breaking with the traditions of the past. The change has, however, been made in most of the larger cities, where the necessity for the change was most pressing.

So far as the state government is concerned, the progress made has been slower even than in the case of the cities. This is due very largely to the fact that while in the case of the cities, old traditions as to the administrative system had crystallized in statutes, in the case of the state, they had crystallized in the state constitutions. Not only were these less easy of amendment than the statutes, but the need of change in the state system

was not as important as in the case of the cities.
Administrative matters there were not as important as in the cities, or at any rate, administrative
inefficiency did not have such disastrous results in
the state government as in the municipal government.

At the same time changes in the old administrative system of the states were necessary, and have
been made. The old system has not, however, as
yet, been transformed as has that of the cities.
Many of our state governments bear evidences of
the influence both of original American administrative ideas, and of the changes occasioned
by the needs of our modern civilization. Thus
in New York we find that the constitution
makes provision both for a class of officers
commonly known as "state officers," who are
still, like the governor, to be elected by the
people of the state, and for another class of officers, who almost all date from later than 1850,
who are in most cases appointed by the governor,
and are to some degree subjected to his direction and supervision.

The tendency in most of the states whose civilization is most complex, is toward administrative
centralization and away from their original unconcentrated administrative conditions.[1] Thus in both

[1] Whitten *op. cit.;* Fairlie *op. cit.*

New York and Massachusetts most of the new fields of administrative activity into which the state government has entered, are occupied solely by the state central administration. If provision is made for the supervision of banking, insurance and transportation companies, and the inspection of factories, it is the state central administration alone which is vested with power. Again, there is a tendency, although it is not very marked as yet, for the state to provide for a central administrative supervision of certain branches of administration formerly left to the uncontrolled management of the local corporations. The most noticeable instances of this tendency are to be found in the assessment of property for the purpose of state taxation, in the school administration, and in the case of public charitable and correctional institutions. State Boards of Equalization, State Superintendents of Schools and Boards of Education, and State Boards of Charities and Prisons are not by any means so uncommon as they were forty or even thirty years ago. Indeed, the desire to free the school administration from the domination of politics takes, in the minds of most educational reformers, the concrete shape of increasing the power of central administrative officers, and by so much diminishing that of the legislature and the local corporations.

In other words, we have almost completely centralized our national administrative system; we
have done much to centralize or concentrate our
municipal administration under the mayor; we
have begun to centralize our state administration
in that many officers are now appointed and
removed by the governor, exercise their powers
independently of local corporations or local officers,
and even in some cases have powers of supervision
over branches of administration still in the hands
of such local corporations or officers. This centralization has come about almost imperceptibly,
and notwithstanding the fact that, as a people, we
are engaged at all times in sounding the praises
of self-government.

The centralization in our national government
has, because it has taken from subordinate officers
the political characteristics which they unquestionably had at one time, resulted in the demand
that they shall be relieved from the political control of the party organization. A somewhat similar demand, though not so emphatic, has been
made in the cities and in the state governments.
This is to be noticed in the case of school-teachers,
and the members of the police and fire departments, and to a less degree in the case of the
clerical and subordinate force generally. Indeed,
it may be said that the demand that these officers

should be taken out of politics was made before the civil service reform movement, in the sense in which these words are popularly used, was begun.

But in all these cases the movement to separate administration from politics — for that is what this development is — did not begin until the old American system of administration had been abandoned and our faces had been turned in the direction of administrative centralization. The first law providing for examinations for entrance into the national civil service was passed in 1853, at about the time it was recognized that the national administrative system was centralized under the President. One of the first instances of the attempt to secure a permanent municipal service is found in the New York charter of 1873. This was adopted almost immediately after the adoption of the principle that the municipal government should be centralized under the mayor. This had been done in the charter of 1870. Not only did the movement not begin until this change was made, but it may be questioned whether it could have begun sooner. For the necessary coördination between the functions of politics and administration could not have been made until the administration had been somewhat centralized. Where no provision is made for such coördination in the governmental system, it must be made outside of it, and this can be done only through the party — only through recognizing the propriety of insisting on political tests for officers charged with executing the law. Such officers under our original decentralized system were not really subject to any governmental control, except such as was to be found in the supervision exercised over them by the courts in the interest of the maintenance of the law. This being insufficient to produce harmony between the making and the execution of the law, had to be supplemented by the control of the political parties. As soon, however, as the administration became somewhat centralized, this control of the political parties became unnecessary, except as to the highest officers, since these could control more fully the actions of their subordinates, and being themselves subject to party control, might bring about the necessary harmony in the governmental system.

This centralization of administration toward which we have gradually, and it would seem irresistibly, tended, appears therefore to involve the recognition of a sphere of government in which politics are to have much less influence than has been accorded to them in the past. The recognition of such a sphere of government is made possible because the necessary political control over administration under the system of administrative centralization may be obtained through the power of the party over the legislature and the officers at the head of the administration. It is also made necessary if we are to hope for any great administrative efficiency, and if the party is to be kept in its proper position, *i.e.* as a means and not an end, an aid and not a hindrance to the expression of the popular will.

The tendency toward administrative centralization should therefore be encouraged and not hindered. We should remember that in our traditional fear of centralization we may have been frightened by a bogie which has been conjured up by designing persons conscious that a proper organization of our administrative system will work to their disadvantage. We should, however, insist that this centralization should be accompanied by a fuller recognition of a sphere of government where the influence of politics is baneful. Insistence upon this point is necessary, both from the point of view of administrative efficiency and from the point of view of the existence of popular government itself.

A centralized administrative system, in which the influence of politics is strong, can easily be

made use of to further the interests of the political
party at the expense of ease in the expression of
the popular will. Centralized administration may
become the instrument in the hands of irresponsible party leaders, if such exist, which will make
impossible both administrative efficiency and popular government. In the history of the United
States the long-continued failure to recognize that
there is an administrative function which, like the
judicial function, should be exercised free from the
influence of politics, has had the result of render-
ing our government less popular than it once was.
The party in control of the governmental offices
has made use of them not merely to influence the
expression of the popular will, but actually to
thwart it when once expressed. Centralization of
administration without the recognition of the necessity for officers who, like judges, should have a
reasonably permanent tenure and of whom impartiality in their actions may be demanded, tends
to increase the influence of party leaders at the
expense of the power of the people to express
their will. Popular government may thus be lost
almost without our knowing it, and without any
important changes in our general form of government. That it has been lost in this way in the
past history of the world cannot be denied. That
it shall not be lost in our own case, depends very

largely on our ability to prevent politics from exercising too great an influence over administration, and the parties in control of the administration from using it to influence improperly the expression of the public will.

CHAPTER VI

In what has already been said, the attempt has
been made to show that the two primary functions
of the state were to express and execute its will,
and that if the expression of this will were to be
something more than a philosophical statement of
belief, a counsel of perfection, there must be a
coördination of these functions, *i.e.* that the execution of the will of the state must be subjected to
the control of the body which expresses it. This
coördination, it has been shown, may be brought
about in the governmental system by subjecting
all administrative officers to the control of a superior governmental authority which is intrusted
ultimately with the expression of the will of the
state. In order that this control may be effective
and may be found in the governmental system, the
administrative system must be considerably centralized. If this coördination of the expression and
the execution of the will of the state is not brought

about in the governmental system, it must be provided for outside of the government. Where it is found outside of the government, it is to be found in the political party. It must of necessity be found there if the administrative system is not considerably centralized and under ultimate and effective legislative control.

If provision is not made for this coördination in the governmental system, the work of the party is much greater than it is where the governmental organization provides for this coördination. Inasmuch as the party organization is in all cases formed in order to do the work which is devolved upon it by the governmental system, the party organization will be much less complicated and much less centralized under a governmental system which is so formed as to permit the body, charged ultimately with the expression of the will of the state, to exercise an effective control over the agents charged with its execution.

To be more concrete, in a governmental system which, like that to be found in the states of the United States, makes higher executive and administrative officers largely independent of the legislature, and inferior administrative officers largely independent of the higher administrative officers, the party organization must be much stronger, much more complicated, and much more centralized than that of England, where the ministers are at the head of the administration, and are responsible to Parliament. In the one case, the parties must not merely make provision for the election of legislative officers, they must see to it, as well, that officers are provided for the execution of the laws, who will work both in harmony with each other and with the legislature. In the other case, they need provide only for the election of legislative officers, leaving to the legislative body the duty of bringing about the necessary harmony between the execution and the making of the law. In the one case, parties in their extra-governmental organization must concern themselves not merely with the function of expressing the will of the state, but also with the function of executing that will; in the other case, they have to do merely with the expression of the state will.

Further, if in a given state the relations of central and local government are such that the localities have largely in their hands the execution of state laws, the state parties must, if they are to discharge their necessary functions, have to do not merely with the expression and execution of the state will by state officers, but also with the execution of that will by local authorities. State parties must, in such a case, concern themselves with local politics. The differentiation of state and local parties, if such differentiation is ever possible, is conditioned upon a differentiation of state and local politics. Such a differentiation is possible only where local bodies cease to act as independent state agents.

Party organization is thus based on the character and amount of the work the party has to do; and the work the party has to do depends very largely on the relations existing both between the different organs of the central government and between the central and the local governments. If the system of government is at the same time unconcentrated from the point of view of the relations of the different departments of the general government, and decentralized from the point of view of the relations of the central and the local governments, the work of the party is very great, and to do this work the party organization must be correspondingly strong and permanent.

But while the necessary political control over the execution of the state will may thus be found outside of the government, and in the party, it is none the less true that a too great extension of this control may, on the one hand, make the execution of the state will inefficient and, on the other, may throw difficulties in the way of its expression. Both these results may, and probably will, follow the failure to recognize a function of administration, as described within these pages, and the partisan use of powers of patronage.

Many have supposed that these evils might be avoided where the political control over the execution of the state will is vested with the party, by endeavoring to keep the party organization weak. The party organization must, however, be strong where the governmental system is not concentrated and not centralized; for in these conditions the party must be looked to to bring about that harmony between the making and execution of the law which is so necessary to orderly and progressive government.

It can further be shown that even where the governmental system is both concentrated and centralized a reasonably strong party system is usually a necessary prerequisite of popular government and efficient administration.

Where the executive is largely independent of the legislature, weak parties are accompanied by methods of government which may not be called popular. Where the executive is dependent on the legislature, weak parties are too apt to be accompanied by inefficient administration.

Thus, in Germany, where the hereditary monarchy has not been made responsible to the legislature, and where the parties are weak, the rôle which the legislature plays is a subordinate one.

It has, as a matter of fact, almost no initiation, while it is notorious that the powers of the Crown are exerted to obtain a complaisant majority in the legislature in order to prevent that body from exercising the powers of veto which it possesses with regard to propositions submitted to it by the Crown. The national parties are so weak as not to be able to "direct or control the government."[1] Why the national parties are so weak does not concern us, but whatever may be the cause of their weakness, the system of government which permits of such conditions may not be called popular.

Where, on the other hand, the executive authority is dependent on the legislature, the existence of strong national parties is just as necessary. The experience of France is proof of this. There, owing to the rather intermittent existence of the legislative body, strong national parties have not been able to develop. A real legislative body of any importance cannot be said to have existed prior to the Revolution. When the Estates General met in 1789, it had not met before for considerably more than a century, and naturally did not even know how it was to proceed to take action. Some of its members thought the Estates should meet separately, others, that they should all as-

[1] Lowell, *op. cit.*, Vol. II., p. 503.

semble together. It was only after it had settled this question that it could act at all. If this was the case in so important a matter, it can well be imagined that its ideas of its more detailed functions were very vague.

Since the meeting of the Estates General in 1789, the existence of a central legislative body in France has not been continuous. There are no strongly organized national parties, such as are to be found in either the United States or England. There are, instead, groups of persons who are accustomed to act together, either based largely on local considerations or owing personal allegiance to some prominent public man. Party allegiance sits very lightly on the shoulders of both people and politicians; and, such as it is, it is owed to a local clique or a man of local influence, rather than to a national party or a man of national reputation. Parties, such as they are, have practically no national organization, draw up no national platforms, and have no really national leaders.[1] The national party leader is practically unknown, and the parties are merely more or less local cliques, which may or may not work together.

Upon such a basis the attempt has been made to build up a system of party government, that is, a system which requires the government to be

[1] Lowell, *op. cit.*, Vol. I., p. 106 *et seq.*

administered by ministers who possess the confidence of the majority of the legislature. The position which the President of the Republic has been obliged to assume, as one who neither reigns nor governs, has made it necessary to develop a minister superior to the others in order that some harmony of action among the ministers may be secured. This minister is known as the President of the Council of Ministers. He differs from the English Prime Minister in that, while the latter is not only a Prime Minister, but also the leader of a national political party in control of the Parliament, the French President of the Council is merely the Prime Minister. He is not the leader of any national political party, simply because there is no such thing. His position toward his colleagues of the ministry is also quite different from that of the English Prime Minister. Instead of being their superior to whom they owe obedience, he is rather in the position of one who is first among equals.

Not being the head of a national party in control of the legislature, the French Prime Minister cannot rely as can the English Prime Minister upon any such thing as party allegiance. But at the same time he and his ministry must keep the confidence of the majority in the legislature. This, translated into plain English, means he must get and keep the votes of a majority. How now does he do this? In the first place, he gets his majority by selecting as his colleagues in the Cabinet men who have a certain personal following, of necessity being obliged largely to disregard the consideration of the question whether they will work in harmony with him. For what he wants is not so much harmony as votes. Harmony he may desire, but votes he must have. But he and his colleagues must not only get a majority; they must also keep it if they would stay in office. This majority is kept together by the grant to the deputies by the ministers of all manner of favors, some of which are perhaps proper, some of which, from the point of view of good government and efficient administration, are decidedly improper. The French administration, being highly centralized, lends itself quite readily to this distribution of favors. But the result of their distribution is greatly to impair administrative efficiency.

The condition of things in Italy is worse even in this respect than in France. This is due to the fact that Italian national unity dates only from 1870. Parties are therefore much more local even than in France, while the administration is quite as highly centralized. The degree to which the efficiency of the administration is impaired by such a system of government is well illustrated by the statement of an Italian politician, at the time when the Italian railroads were owned and operated by the government, that the government was unable to operate fast trains because of the demands made by the deputies that all trains should stop at almost all stations in the districts from which they were elected. These demands the ministers could not refuse for fear of losing votes.[1] The efficiency of administration under such a system of government is impaired also by the fact that each minister must of necessity work in his own interest rather than in that of the party, party responsibility having largely given place to individual responsibility. A harmonious ministerial policy thus becomes difficult if not impossible.

The French and Italian party systems, if what they have can be dignified by the name of party systems, are thus based upon the most sordid of motives, that of self-interest. The Prime Minister chooses the members of his Cabinet, not because they owe allegiance to the party to which he belongs or because they hold the same ideas as to things political which he holds. He chooses them because he wants the votes which he believes they control. They in their turn have a political following, not because they represent certain political

[1] Lowell, *op. cit.*, Vol. I., p. 219.

principles, but because they are in a position to distribute favors in return for political support.

The deputies controlled by these party leaders finally owe their election not to any appeal to the party allegiance of their constituents. They owe their election to their personal popularity. This popularity has been obtained very largely because of past favors granted or future favors promised. One of the most common complaints in France is "that the deputies represent local and personal interests rather than national ones." [1]

The extent to which the French deputy is the personal rather than the political representative of his constituents, is illustrated by an account which two deputies gave at a public dinner some years ago of the letters they received from their districts. "Some constituents wanted their representative to go shopping for them; others asked him to consult a physician in their behalf; and more than one begged him to procure a wet nurse, hearing that this could be done better in Paris than in the provinces." [2]

Such a condition of things is not conceivable in that part of American political life in which the influence of national parties is predominant. Such

---

[1] Lowell, *op. cit.*, Vol. I., p. 136

[2] *Ibid.* quoting from Scherer, *La Démocratie et la France*, pp. 34, 35.

a condition of things does, however, actually obtain in the United States where, as is the case in its largest cities, the dominant political organizations are primarily local parties, and only secondarily local organizations of the national party. Here the following of the average politician is due to his personal popularity rather than to the fact that he represents a party.

The local politician is very commonly something in the nature of a fairy godfather to his constituents. He it is who bails them out of the police courts, if, perchance, a cruel fate has led them within its portals. He it is who lends them money if they are behind in their rent, enables them to get their share of the coal which the city distributes among the worthy poor, and gets the head of the family, when out of work, a place in the city service, or with some one of the many corporations seeking favors from the city government.

This classic relation of patron and client, or if one prefers, this mediæval and feudal relation of lord and vassal, seems bound to arise if party allegiance is seriously impaired. Being based as it is on the sordid motive of self-interest, it cannot itself be the basis of any broad-minded action for the public welfare, and is rather more likely than the most besotted partisan spirit to lead to the misuse of all governmental power in the interest of class or for personal advantage.

It is, of course, true that strongly organized national political parties are made use of by designing persons for the furtherance of corrupt and selfish ends. It is also true that such parties become at times mere machines, whose main purpose is self-perpetuation, not perhaps so much as a means for the accomplishment of the ends for which they were originally formed, as to afford party leaders and their immediate followers opportunities for self-advancement. At the same time, under ordinary conditions, strongly organized national parties stand for the realization in political life of principles whose realization is deemed proper and possible by a large part of the population.

The candidates of strong national parties owe allegiance primarily to the party, and only secondarily to their immediate constituents. While, if elected, they may be expected to work for the local interests of the sections from which they come, and, it may be, for the personal interests of their constituents, their main work is expected to be, and really is, the furtherance of the principles embodied in their party platform. The demands made upon the executive by the political parties for the improper use of executive powers are made not entirely from selfish motives, but in large part in order that the party may be perpetuated, and that the principles that it represents may thereby be realized.

In the case of strong national parties there is after all some motive other than self-interest which leads to political action.   In theory, at least, party allegiance is due to motives more or less ideal, however much practice may depart from the theory. In the case of local parties, which we are urged sometimes to put in the place of national parties, the basis of party cohesion is quite the reverse of the ideal.   It is, on the contrary, grossly material.

The destruction or the serious weakening of strong national parties in our unconcentrated and decentralized system of government would not thus seem to be advisable.   It is true that as organized and operating in the United States political parties are accompanied by serious evils.   But to substitute for them political organizations bound more or less loosely together by the bonds of personal allegiance to local party leaders would, if we may judge not only from French and Italian experience but as well from our own experience in our largest cities, be the height of folly.

Some other means than the destruction or even the serious weakening of these parties must be resorted to.   Enough has already been said to show that the most serious evils by which our party system is accompanied are administrative inefficiency and lack of responsiveness of the popular will. The attempt has already been made to show that administrative efficiency can be obtained only as a result of the recognition of the existence of an administrative function which should be discharged free from the influences of politics. The recognition of such a function of government in the United States may be facilitated by a reasonable centralization of the administrative system accompanied by a greater permanence in the tenure of administrative officers. How now may the political parties be made more responsive to the public will? The endeavor to answer this question will be made in the succeeding chapters.

CHAPTER VII

POPULAR GOVERNMENT

POPULAR government has unquestionably been the political ideal of the nineteenth century. Its realization has been the end of most of the changes which have been made during the century in the political institutions of nations enjoying western European civilization. This is seen in the steadily increasing participation of the people in the work of government, accorded by the constitutions which have been adopted, the laws which have been passed, and the extra-governmental and extra-constitutional devices to which resort has been had. In all the western European countries, including within them the United States, which possess written constitutions, the newer constitutions, and in England, which has no such instrument, the statutes of Parliament, have widened the suffrage.

The frame of government itself has been so changed, either by constitutional provision or by extra-constitutional device, as to give the people themselves or the people's representatives greater control over the actual conduct of government. In England the establishment of cabinet government has made the House of Commons, the representative of the people, the controlling governmental authority. In the United States the nomination of the President by the party conventions has brought the choice of the President one degree nearer the people than was originally contemplated by the Constitution.

And yet, notwithstanding that popular government has thus been the ideal of the nineteenth century, few of the persons who hold this ideal have a clear idea of what popular government in its concrete manifestations really is. It is unquestionably true that most persons regard popular government as a system of government in which decisions as to political conduct are the result of the conscious deliberations of the people. It is, however, just as unquestionably true that the forms of government which we are accustomed to regard as popular, and which are to be found in conditions of life at all complex, do not generally provide for any such conscious deliberation on the part of the people.

Where conditions of life are at all complex, *i.e.* where the population is numerous and not thoroughly homogeneous, where the territory to be governed is extended and the distribution of wealth and intelligence is not comparatively equal, the necessities of the case have developed along-side of the formal governmental system more or less voluntary extra-governmental organizations, which exercise a controlling influence on the formal governmental system.   As Mr. Lowell points out, " A superficial glance at the history of democracy ought to be enough to convince us that in a great nation the people as a whole do not and cannot really govern.   The fact is that we are ruled by parties whose action is more or less modified, but never completely directed, by public opinion . . . always more or less warped by the existence of party ties."[1]   Parties, although formed to secure certain ends, get to be ends in and of themselves. Party allegiance gets to replace, as a primary motive of conduct, adherence to political principle. The perpetuation of the party often appears more important than the ends for whose attainment the party itself originally was formed.

Party leaders, on account of this important position assumed by the parties, often assume more importance as controlling factors in the political system than governmental officers.   The aims of these party leaders must in large degree be the same as the aims of the party which they lead.   They must strive in first instance for the

[1] Vol. I., p. 69.

perpetuation of the party. For the party is the instrument through which the ends for which the party was formed can be attained. The maintaining in its integrity and power of the party organization and the preservation of successful party leadership are so necessary to the attainment of the ultimate ends of the party that the rôle of the members of the party ceases to be the positive determination of the party policy, and is reduced to the amendment or negativing of propositions made by the party leaders. A body in which all shades of opinion exist and find expression is apt to be a debating society merely, incapable of positive action. But parties are formed for action rather than debate. They must accomplish something positive in the world of action. They must therefore follow rather than lead, and in order that they may follow they must have leaders capable of originating a policy which will approve itself to the party membership.

Now, in order that government under parties shall be popular, conditions must be such, both that the party, in whom the people as a whole do not have confidence, shall retire from the active control of the government, and that party leaders who in like manner have forfeited the confidence of the party shall retire from active control of the party. If these conditions do not exist, the system of government cannot be said to be popular. If they do exist, the government is probably as nearly popular as government ever has been or ever can be expected to be in any except the most primitive and simple social conditions. Certainly in the governments of states, possessing a highly developed civilization, with which we are acquainted, the people as a whole have had no greater influence on the conduct of public affairs. England, whose government may, perhaps, with the exceptions of the United States and Switzerland, be regarded as the most popular in existence, is a good example of this fact.

When, after the struggles of the seventeenth century, Parliament came to be regarded as the supreme authority in the English government, no attempt was made by that body to carry on the government in the sense that it was to formulate a policy to be executed by the Crown. On the contrary, Parliament was content to play the subordinate rôle of approving or disapproving a policy formulated by the Crown.[1] The attempt made by William III. to obtain the approval of his policy by Parliament through choosing as his ministers persons who had its confidence, soon led, under sovereigns less strong and less able, to Parliament's

[1] Such is the present condition in Germany, where strong parties have not developed.

dictating to the Crown whom it should appoint as its ministers. As Mr. Lowell remarks,[1] "The system which had been devised in order that the king might control the House of Commons became, therefore, the means by which the House of Commons through its leaders controlled the king, and thus all the powers of the House of Commons and the Crown became vested in the same men, who guided legislation and took charge of administration at the same time."

This relegation of the Crown to the position of one who reigned but did not govern did not, however, result, as might at first be supposed, in the adoption of the principle that the popular body could formulate policies to be executed by its servants. For, as Mr. Lowell says, the ministers not only "took charge of the administration," but also "guided legislation." It might be added that they also, as a result of their party leadership, do much in the election campaigns to determine the membership of the House of Commons whose legislation as ministers and members of that body they guide.

Of course the present position of the ministers as leaders at the same time of legislation and administration was not at once worked out. But just so soon as this position was determined, and

[1] *Op. cit.*, Vol. I., p. 4.

the localities in the kingdom, through the process of administrative centralization which has been going on through this century, had been subordinated to the central government, the ministers became heirs to all the old powers of the English Crown, the recognized sovereign of the English people, and as such sovereign, from the legal point of view exercising all powers of government.

At the present time the ministers unite in their hands powers of legislation and powers of administration with regard to both the central and local governments. They both formulate policies and execute them after their formulation ; and so long as their action meets with the approval of Parliament whose representatives they are, there is none to gainsay them. If, however, they fail to gain such approval, in accordance with constitutional practice, they must resign. their powers to others whose policy is approved by Parliament. Finally, in order to make Parliament representative of the people, who in greater and greater numbers have been given the suffrage, the ministers are permitted to appeal from the decisions of Parliament to the people ; while Parliament itself, in case no such appeal was taken, is accustomed to dissolve of its own accord at least once in seven years.

In this way the entire English government is

made responsible to Parliament, which in its turn
is responsible to the people. Such a system of
government requires for its successful working the
existence of reasonably strong and coherent parties,
whose leaders are the ministers of the government
when their party is in power. It does not, however, make nearly the demands on the party that
are made by the American system of government.
The necessary coördination of the expression and
execution of the will of the state is obtained in,
not outside of, the governmental system. Further,
while no attempt is made in such a system to
adopt the democratic ideal, as it has been described, that is to assure to the people or their
representatives the formulation of policies whose
execution is intrusted to ministerial subordinates,
the system does secure to the representatives of
the people and to the people as a whole the power
to say nay to a policy of which they do not
approve, and does insure that in case of the
expression of such disapproval the persons in
charge of the government shall give way to others
more in accord with the popular mind.

This is insured by the simplicity of the system.
It is insured also almost without the sanction of
law as we are accustomed to use the term. The
Cabinet, which is the body producing the necessary coördination, is a body absolutely unknown to

the law; the names of its members are never officially published; its meetings are quite unofficial, no record whatever being kept of its proceedings.

Not only has the development of the Cabinet been extra-legal, it has in the past been regarded as illegal. Protest after protest was made against its assumption of power. It was called a cabal, and was accused of subverting the constitutional principles of English government.[1] But notwithstanding all that has been said against it, it has continued to develop until it has become the real keystone of the arch of British politics. That it was able to develop as it did, was probably due to the fact that the English governmental system is flexible as is perhaps no other. Its form is fixed only by statutes which may be changed by Parliament. The courts cannot protect it, and changes are made in it almost imperceptibly. A governmental organ may be made to discharge functions for which it was not intended, or may be made to act in a way not originally anticipated; and if such action is not protested against, it is regarded as a precedent, and, owing to the Englishman's traditional regard for precedent, soon comes to be regarded as a part of the Constitution.

[1] Todd, *Parliamentary Government in Great Britain*, Vol. II., p. 93 *et seq.*

That such a political system is, in the case of the English people, an admirable one, can hardly be doubted. It permits the development of government along the lines of least resistance, and therefore along the most natural lines. It permits, further, political development within the governmental organization, or at any rate in close connection with it, and has the great advantage of insuring responsibility, since persons whom the law can reach, that is, persons holding official position, are the persons actually exercising political powers. The fact that political responsibility is, comparatively speaking, easily fixed, that the people may force out of power political leaders who do not possess their confidence, makes the whole system one in which popular government is easily secured. For the party is made responsible and the leaders of the party who are the leaders of the government are responsible. The responsible character of the government makes the whole political system a responsible one.

The condition of things in this country is from the formal and theoretical point of view much the same as in England. Indeed, if anything, the formal American system of government would seem to assure greater popular responsibility than the English. The formal American executive is not hereditary as is the English Crown. Both houses of the American legislature have their origin in a direct or indirect popular vote, while membership in the English House of Lords is inherited.

The actual political conditions in America do not, however, permit of as great popular responsibility upon the part of the government as is secured by the actual political conditions in England. When the governments of the states of the United States were formed they evidenced the influence of the democratic ideal to which cohesion has been made. That is, they were organized in such a way that questions of policy were to be determined by popular representative bodies — the legislatures — which were elected by a comparatively large number of people. These bodies not merely had the power to veto proposals made to them by the executive, but also themselves initiated policies, all the details of which they themselves determined. These policies were to be put into execution by other organs of government regarded as servants of the legislature, but on account of their independent position not really subject to an effective legislative control.

Now while the ideal of democracy was realized in the formal governmental systems thus established in the states, it was an ideal which was not realized in actual political practice. This ideal was not realized, although the form of government based upon it continued in existence. That it was not realized was due to the character of the political party organization through which the government came to be carried on.

The earliest records we have of the organization and action of the political parties which were in existence at the time of the establishment of our state governments show that, notwithstanding the democratic forms of government, the actual determination of the popular will was very largely controlled by a few people, who, by shrewd manipulation, and in some cases by questionable practices, succeeded in forcing or persuading the voters to follow their lead.

In describing the pre-revolutionary caucus, Gordon[1] says: "It [*i.e.* the word "caucus"] seems to mean a number of persons, whether more or less, met together to consult upon, adopt, and prosecute some scheme of policy. The word is not of novel invention. More than fifty years ago Mr. Samuel Adams's father and twenty others, one or two from the north end of town, where all the ship business is gathered, used to meet, make a caucus, and lay their plans for introducing certain persons into certain places of trust and power.

[1] *History of the American Revolution*, 3d American edition, Vol. I., p. 240, note; quoted from Dallinger: *Nominations for Elective Office*, p. 8.

When they had settled it, they separated, and used each their particular influence within their own circle. He and his friends would furnish themselves with ballots, including the names of the parties fixed upon, which they distributed on the day of election. By acting in concert with a careful and extensive distribution of ballots they generally carried the elections to their own mind. In like manner it was that Mr. Samuel Adams first became a representative for Boston."

This party system did not, however, fulfil the ideals of democracy, and the attempt was made almost everywhere in this country to democratize the party machinery, so that it might in its outward manifestations conform to the ideals of democracy as expressed in the form of government which had been adopted. The party organization was, therefore, almost everywhere remodelled. The party voters everywhere insisted that meetings should be held at which all of the members of the party might be present and act in the nomination of candidates, or in the election of delegates to act for them in conventions established for districts which were too large to permit of the direct action of the party members in the nomination of candidates.

Senator Dallinger says, in his excellent book, already referred to :[1] " By the beginning of the

[1] p. 12.

Revolution, the caucus or primary had become pretty well established in New England and the Middle States. With the close of the war it gradually lost its secret character which had been rendered necessary by the exigencies of the time, and became a miniature town meeting of the party voters of the ward or district. In New England, except in some of the large cities, and in those sections of the country settled by New England people, the caucus still retains its original town meeting character. But in the other states with the growth of population the "primary" has come to be a mere polling-place for the election of delegates to the various conventions and of members of the local party committee, there being no opportunity whatever for any discussion of the merits of the various candidates. The inevitable result has been that the real work of nomination has largely fallen either into the hands of 'parlor caucuses,'[1] or of political committees and clubs — the power of the individual voter being restricted to the choice between candidates agreed upon at such preliminary secret conferences or named by such organizations."

[1] "The reader is not to infer that there are no parlor caucuses in New England; but where the caucus is a small body and opportunity is afforded for popular discussion of the merits of candidates, there is always a chance of breaking a 'slate' of a previous parlor caucus which does not exist where the primary is only a polling-place."

The result of the development of party organization in the United States has been that, notwithstanding the democratic form of the government and the likewise formally democratic character of the party organization, the political functions of the ordinary individual are confined to saying "Yes" or "No" to propositions made to him relative to the nomination or election of persons proposed for political or party office by those in control of the party organization. The only instances where the voters of the party have positive initiation in the determination of who shall be the party candidates are, according to Senator Dallinger, in the rural districts of New England. Here the primary or caucus is described as "a miniature town meeting of the party voters," where "opportunity is afforded for public discussion of the merits of candidates," and "there is always a chance of breaking a 'slate' made at a previous parlor caucus." The reason why these exceptional conditions are found in the rural districts of New England is not far to seek. There we find both the conditions most favorable to the development of democracy, and a local-government system which almost from the beginning of the history of the country has accustomed the people as a whole to participate in politics. But even here it is to be noticed that the parlor caucus is not unknown, and the actual form of political action may consist rather in breaking than in making a slate.

Actual political conditions in the United States thus resemble actual political conditions in England in that the people have little positive power in formulating and putting into execution their ideas relative to political conduct.

Does the American system, however, resemble the English system in allowing the people both to retire from power a party in which they do not have confidence, and to retire from party leadership a party leader when they have ceased to approve of his policy?

If we consider this question merely from the point of view of the governmental system, we must at once admit that the American system is not of such a character as to admit of as immediate responsiveness to the public will as is assured by the English system. Cabinet government, whatever may be its defects, does assure the possibility of at once finding out what is public opinion, so far as that is represented in Parliament, and of making that opinion effective. Presidential government, as our system has been called, makes this impossible on account of the independent position of the executive. Differences between the legislative and the executive cannot be settled until the time fixed by the Constitution for the general elections. The fact that the legislature and the executive are elected in different ways makes it possible for such differences to exist immediately after the election. The governmental system being fixed in a written constitution cannot be changed by custom. Constitutional amendment is, in our experience, a slow and almost impossible method of political growth.

The parties have had to develop extraordinary strength in order to be able to bring about harmony in the government. They had not merely to be very strong, they had also to be quite permanent, for they had to strive to control all branches of the government for quite a long period of time if they were to hope to see realized in political conduct the principles for which they were formed. Notwithstanding this strength and permanence, parties are only partially successful in doing the work devolved upon them by the American governmental system. There are too many instances of governmental deadlocks in our political life to permit us to believe that the efforts of parties have been absolutely successful.

This great strength, this comparative permanence, which it is necessary that parties should have in order to do the work devolved upon them by the formal governmental system, have unquestionably caused the party organizations to be less responsive to the party will than is desirable. The individual members of the party have not only not been able to make the party leaders as responsive as might be wished, they have not desired to insist upon as full a measure of responsibility from party leaders as is desirable from their fear of weakening the party. This unwillingness on their part is in large measure due to their appreciation of the enormous task which our governmental system devolves upon the party, and to the feeling that the accomplishment of this task makes necessary that they evince willingness to forego a part of their political privileges, if through such action the party to which they have attached themselves can be successful in obtaining control of the government. As in the case of national danger, the citizen is willing to pardon a degree of arbitrary action on the part of the government to which he would not submit in times of peace, so in face of the bitter political warfare which the American system of government would seem to promote, the party members will submit to action on the part of party leaders which in a more tranquil condition of things they would not hesitate to resent.

The American political system as at present existing does not thus satisfy the demands of popular government, as they have been defined, in as full a measure as is desirable. It does not in the first place permit the easy retirement, from the control of public affairs, of a party which has lost the confidence of the people. It does not in the second place give the party members, in case they disapprove of policies proposed by party leaders, the power to bring about as easily as is desirable a change in party leadership.

If it be said that the electorate makes our governmental system popular, it may be answered that the power the people practically have at an election is merely to choose between several candidates, none of whom they may desire, and who, if elected, do not have the power always to secure the adoption of the popular policy. What the people should have, if the government is to be really popular in character, is the power at a given time to force an unpopular party out of the control of the government, and to oblige the party leaders in whom they do not have confidence to lay down their rights of leadership, giving place to others more in accord with the public will. Until such a condition of things is reached, either within the government or the party, no government can be regarded as popular.

That the English method of securing such a result, so far as may be, in the governmental organization, has great advantages, is not to be denied, although it may, of course, be doubted whether such a method would be applicable in this country. It may be that we shall have to get the same thing outside of our governmental system, and in our parties. The discontent with party management and the recent growth of the independent voting class would indicate that the people are gradually becoming aware that our real political system is not what an examination of our governmental system would at first lead an observer of it to think it is. The growing interest in methods of primary reform indicates, further, that the conviction is gaining ground that the point of attack by those who believe in the preservation of popular government is not so much the formal governmental system as the party organization.

CHAPTER VIII

THE BOSS

THE American political system has been characterized not merely by the development of strong and highly centralized parties; of recent years it has also become more and more apparent that these parties both in their state and local organizations have fallen or are falling under the control of a single person. Most Americans who give much thought to political questions in the broad sense which may be applied to these words, regard this tendency or movement — for it would seem to be merely a tendency in some parts of the country, and sufficiently marked in others to be called a movement — as an extremely unfortunate one, and as presaging the destruction of popular government. Indeed, the affection of the average American for his conception of popular government is so great that probably few if any of the persons who have attained great prominence as party leaders could be elected to any office in the gift of the American people. Conscious of this feeling

among the people, it is seldom the case that such
party leaders make use of their unquestioned power
in the party organizations to secure nominations
for elective offices, preferring to take only those
offices in search of which they will not be obliged
to run the gauntlet of a popular vote. In other
cases they prefer to occupy no official position at
all, either in the government or it may be in the
formal party organization. Notwithstanding this
astonishing modesty on their part, it is perfectly
well known throughout the community that their
actual powers are most extensive. Like the cen-
turion in the Scriptures they say to each of their
servants both within and without the government,
"'Do this,' and he doeth it."

When it is remembered that it is the party which
controls both the legislature and the administration, and it is the party leader or "boss," as we
have accustomed ourselves to call him, who controls the party, it will at once be seen what a com-
manding position is accorded by the American
political system to the bosses. These uncrowned
kings, although they neither reign, nor often, so
far as the outward forms are concerned, govern,
are still one of the most if not the most important
factor in the formally democratic and popular government of the United States. They control the
making of laws and their execution after they are

made.   As Mr. Horace E. Deming has said : " The deliberative functions of the legislature as conceived by the 'fathers' have absolutely ceased to exist for many purposes.   It registers as automatically the will of a third party and as little the results of its own deliberations as the Electoral College.   The form of a legislature survives, but the substance and the spirit have vanished. . . . The legislative power . . . is exercised by one man or a small self-constituted group through dummies who are still in name representatives of the people."

What is here said of the making of law may be said with equal propriety of the enforcement of law.   In more than one large city in this country the people elect a mayor who has wide powers of appointment.   But this mayor after his election exercises those powers apparently in accordance with the commands of the boss who, through his control of the party machinery, gave such mayor his nomination.

That the foregoing is an accurate description of the operations of government in many parts of the United States, few will deny.   The question which presents itself to the impartial student of government is not so much how this condition of things came about, or whether it is consistent with our ideals of democratic government.   It is rather,

Is this a natural, and to that extent presumably an inevitable, development?

To answer this question we must ask ourselves still further what exactly is the position of the boss as we see him. Is he merely a political leader or is he something more? Nor must we in our investigation be prejudiced against the boss because he does not conform to democratic ideals. For the democratic ideal may be an improper one; that is, it may be based on an incorrect conception of human nature, or it may be unsuited to anything short of the ideal conditions of human life, — conditions which are certainly not now at hand, and which can be expected to exist only after many more centuries of struggle and progress.

In the same way the means which the boss uses to obtain or keep his power should not exercise too great an influence on our ideas as to the propriety of the existence of the boss. For political development has generally been accomplished by making use of the means which were at hand without a too nice discrimination as to their propriety, when considered from the point of view of individual morality. By this statement it is not intended to convey the impression that immoral political methods are not to be reprobated, but rather that all political development has been

accomplished by means which will not bear investigation. We are too often apt to forget that it is
really the good which men do that lives after them,
Shakespeare to the contrary notwithstanding.
Many political institutions which find their origin
in actions really iniquitous are later regarded as
most beneficial. Human progress gives many examples of such, of which the historian alone knows
the evil of their conception. It is frequently the
case that the Lord maketh the wrath of man to
praise him. As Mr. Ford points out, " In the politics of the English race," and it might perhaps be
added in that of all races, " ethical theory does not
control practice in public affairs any more than
in ordinary business. Their institutions have not
been made by rule, but have grown, having their
roots in race motive and taking their characteristic
shape from circumstances of development. In the
fulness of time it appears that this growth has had
a moral order of its own, but the discovery comes
from the appreciation of posterity, and furious
censure is apt to be the lot of those whose activities
sustained the process of that growth which a later
age admires. For all that, there never have been
lacking statesmen of the stuff to endure whatever
obloquy the discharge of the practical duties of
their office may incur."[1] If we bear this thought in

[1] Ford, *Rise and Growth of American Politics*, p. 84.

mind it may perhaps be possible to look at the
boss quite objectively and merely as a political
phenomenon which is worthy of study.

What, then, is the boss? The boss is, in the
first place, the kind of political leader which the
American party system has developed. No one
will question that this is the fact. The American
party system has been already considered. It is
a system which on account of the lack in the governmental system of any effective political control
over the organs provided for the execution of the
will of the state, and on account of the presence
of an extremely decentralized administrative organization, has been obliged to do much work which
in most governmental systems is done in the government. This work has been vastly increased by
the mere fact of the great number of officers to be
elected and because of the prominence given to the
legislature — a body which in the nature of things
is very irresponsible, and if not held in firm control would degenerate into a mere debating society,
incapable of efficient action. The enormous work
thrown on the party by such a system has resulted,
as has been shown, in the development within the
party of a remarkably strong organization. The
centre of political influence has been shifted from
the government to the party. The strength and
permanence of the party organization have resulted

in its being from a political point of view somewhat irresponsible.

This brings us to the question of the irresponsibility of the boss. The mere fact that the boss is a political leader of great influence and power is a matter which to the student of politics is of very little importance. It is merely indicative of the trend which is noticeable in the development of almost all political systems. But that the boss is irresponsible is a much more serious matter. For power without responsibility is a thing against which the human race has been fighting since its first attempts at political organization. The frank recognition of the necessity of political leadership is one thing. The actual existence of irresponsible political leadership is quite another.

The actual irresponsibility of the American boss to the people is probably, however, somewhat exaggerated. It is very often the case that persons disappointed in their political efforts ascribe their failures to incorrect causes and regard the success of those opposed to them as due to the evil machinations of irresponsible leaders, when in reality it may be due to popular support. At the same time it is true, as it has more than once been pointed out, that the American political system does not make the fixing of responsibility easy.

The mere fact that the formal governmental

system is of such a character as not to admit of
clearly defined responsibility for governmental
policy on the part of any governmental officer,
tends to make difficult the formation of any responsible government at all. For responsibility,
if it is to be found at all, must be found outside of
the government and in the party which largely
reflects the conditions existing in the government.
The governmental system of checks and balances,
whatever its advantages may be from other points
of view, makes it difficult for the electors to hold
public officers to account. For it is almost impossible under it to fix the blame or award the credit
for any concrete thing that is done or left undone
by the officers of the government. The electors
must, therefore, look to the party, and within the
party customs exist and practices are followed
which are not permitted for an instant in the government, but which are tolerated in the party
because the people feel instinctively that the party
is, under our present system, almost the only protection against anarchy, the only means of progress.

Admitting, then, that the party is irresponsible,
and that the party leader — the boss — is consequently irresponsible, the question naturally arises,
What may be done to make both the party and the
boss responsible ? In order to answer this question,
it will be advisable to consider somewhat at length

both the way in which the party leader has developed in those countries in which he is to be found, and also what is the method which has been devised in such countries to make him responsible.

Parliamentary government has exhibited two quite distinct types. In the one, of which Germany is an example, the Crown not merely reigns, but governs as well, and the position of the Parliament or popular body is, as has been said, merely that of a body which may only veto or amend propositions made by this governing authority, the Crown. The function of parties in such a system is, as Mr. Lowell says[1] of the German parties, "negative rather than positive, they do not direct or control the government, but simply criticise and amend its measures." In such a system adverse criticism and even a positive veto of propositions made by the political leaders of the nation — the Crown and its ministers — does not result in a change of leadership. In this form of parliamentary government there is no need of the party leader, as the party really has no initiation. The boss, or leader, in the government is to be found in the governmental organization, which, through the Crown and its ministers, makes ample provision for leadership.

In the other form of parliamentary government,

[1] *Op. cit.* II., p. 503.

of which England is an example, not only does the Crown merely reign and not govern, but those who do govern are the ministers selected nominally by the Crown and in reality by the minister "sent for" by the Crown to form a ministry, and obliged by custom to be in harmony with the majority in the House of Commons. The person whom the Crown thus selects, though in theory selected by the Crown in its discretion, is in reality the person who, by reason of his political ability, has come to be recognized as the leader of the party in the majority in the House of Commons. The persons whom he selects as colleagues, though also in theory chosen by the Crown in its discretion, are in reality those persons in either house of Parliament whose presence in the ministry will add the most strength to the "government," as the ministry is apt to be called.[1]

It has been said that the practice of thus selecting ministers who are in accord with each other originated with William III., who selected those persons as ministers from whom he hoped for the greatest aid in controlling Parliament. This prac-

[1] It is not by accident that the term "government" has been applied to the English ministry, and the term "administration" to that of the United States. For the one through its control of Parliament makes as well as administers laws ; the other merely administers laws made by Congress. The one expresses as well as executes the will of the state ; the other merely executes it.

tice resulted finally in subjecting the Crown to the control of Parliament, which, through these ministers responsible to it, assumes the charge of both legislation and administration.   For if the conduct of the government is not satisfactory to it, it expresses its dissatisfaction, and thus forces the ministers to resign.   The responsibility of the government, in the English sense of the word, to the Parliament is complete, and if Parliament is responsible to the people, the responsibility of the government as a whole to the people is also complete.

When this form of government first began to develop, however, Parliament was not by any means responsible even to the small electorate which then existed, nor did ministers always act with that harmony which has since become characteristic of the English Cabinet.   The representative character of Parliament and the harmony of the Cabinet were worked out slowly and in such close connection with the development of the party leader, the "boss," that the supposition is reasonable that the popular government which England possesses is based on its party government, while its party government is based on the boss.

While eventually the system of government adopted by William III. resulted in the subjection of the Crown to the Parliament, at first the efforts of those who were honored by the Crown with portfolios were very largely directed toward making the Parliament subservient to the Crown, as the Crown intended it should be. The attempt was made to accomplish this purpose through the use of means which we of the present day would not hesitate to declare corrupt. There seems to be no question that patronage and money were used freely during the eighteenth century and the early part of the nineteenth century by the Crown and its ministers. The whole municipal organization was prostituted, first by the Crown, and, as the Crown during the reigns of George I. and George II. gradually stepped out of active participation in the government, by the party leaders, in the interest of securing a majority in the House of Commons.

The origin of the modern English press, which has become important as a means of moulding public opinion, is to be found in the efforts of the various party leaders to sway the voting class in their favor.[1]

[1] Mr. Porritt says, in "The Government and the Newspaper Press in England," in the *Political Science Quarterly*, Vol. XII., p. 669: "While the old form of journalism lasted, it was an expensive one for the government, for the one-man journals made no pretence of paying their way. From 1731 to 1742, over £50,000 were paid out by the Walpole government to authors and printers

The use of what would now be called corrupt means to obtain a subservient Parliament, while first introduced by the Crown, was, as has been indicated, by no means abandoned when the Crown abdicated in favor of Parliament. The struggle ceased to be one between Crown and Parliament, and became one between the two great parties that were beginning to crystallize, for the control of Parliament, and through Parliament of the government. Indeed, it may be doubted if corruption was as general and extended while the struggle was between the Crown and Parliament as it was afterward.

Green[1] says of the period beginning with the accession of George I. : " Nor were coarser means of controlling Parliament neglected. The wealth of the Whig houses was lavishly spent in securing a monopoly of the small and corrupt constituencies which made up a large part of the borough representation. It was spent yet more unscrupulously in parliamentary bribery. Corruption was older than Walpole, or the Whig ministers, for it sprang out of the very transfer of power to the House of Commons, which had begun with the

of *Free Britons, Daily Courants, Gazetteers,* and such journals; and in the *Anecdotes of Chatham* there is a statement that during the first three years of George III. £30,000 were expended on the writing and printing of similar publications."

[1] *History of the English People,* Vol. IV., p. 125.

Restoration. The transfer was complete, and the House of Commons was supreme in the state; but while freeing themselves from the control of the Crown, it was as yet imperfectly responsible to the people. It was only at election time that a member felt the pressure of public opinion. The secrecy of parliamentary proceedings, which had been needful as a safeguard against royal interference with debate, served as a safeguard against interference on the part of constituencies. This strange union of immense power with absolute freedom from responsibility brought about its natural results in the bulk of the members. A vote was too valuable to be given without recompense, and parliamentary support had to be bought by places, pensions, and bribes in hard cash."

It was in this soil, fruitful in its corruption, that the English popular boss grew. The person who watered the seed sown as a result of the development of the Cabinet system, was Sir Robert Walpole. He it was who, as far as any one man may be said to have originated any political institution, originated the English boss. As in all other similar cases, his success was due in part to favorable conditions, — conditions indeed which would seem to have made the development of the boss inevitable, — in part, as well to his consummate ability in the management of men. Under two successive kings, and despite persistent and often factious opposition from political rivals, he maintained himself at the head of the English government.

Walpole, while having the welfare of England at heart and while following the wisest policy which England could have pursued in the trying period of her history in which he lived, was, so far as concerned the means used to keep himself in power, quite the reverse of the idealist. As Green says of him : " His prosaic good sense turned sceptically away from the poetic and passionate sides of human feeling, and appeals to the loftier or purer motives of action he laughed at as ' schoolboy flights.' For young members who talked of public virtue or patriotism he had one good-natured answer, ' You will soon come off that and grow wiser.' "   His celebrated remark with regard to certain members of Parliament, " They are all men who have their price," is indicative of his estimate of the kind of human nature with which his political life brought him into contact and of the motives to which he felt sure he could appeal. He took little heed of the charges of corruption brought against him, saying in one of his speeches : " The stale argument of corruption shall never have any weight with me; it has been the common refuge of the disappointed and disaffected ever since government had a being; and it is an accusation which, like all other charges, though unsupported by proof, if advanced against the best and most disinterested administration, and pushed with a becoming violence, a pretended zeal for the public good, will never fail to meet applause among the populace." [1]

But the cynicism which was characteristic both of Walpole's disposition and his public utterances, and the corruption by which he carried on his government could not fail to arouse opposition in a people whose moral sense was not absolutely dead. During a large part of his career this opposition, which, probably because of its futility in producing practical results, was, as Green says of it, "more factious and unprincipled than has ever disgraced English politics," was carried on by a combination of "sorehead" office-seekers, the self-styled "Patriots," on the one hand, and idealists, called by Walpole the "Boys," on the other, led respectively by Pulteney and William Pitt. The opposition was directed not merely to Walpole's policy and methods, but also, and very largely, to his attempts to grasp in his own hands all the powers of government.

According to Clarendon, who wrote somewhat

[1] Coxe, *Life of Sir Robert Walpole*, Vol. III., p. 129.

earlier than the time of Walpole, the idea of a
Prime Minister was very unpopular in England.[1]
Even Walpole himself resented as late as 1741
the title of Prime Minister as an imputation.[2]   In
that same year "a motion was made in the House
of Lords for an address to the king praying him
to 'dismiss Sir Robert Walpole from his presence
and councils forever.'   In this debate it was
vaguely asserted that Walpole had made himself
for the past fifteen or sixteen years 'sole minister.'
But this accusation was combated by the Lord
Chancellor (Hardwicke), on the ground that it was
an impeachment of the king's impartiality to suppose that he could permit any man or minister
solely to engross his ear."[3]   "The motion was
negatived by a large majority.   A protest was
afterward entered on the Journals signed by
thirty-one peers, who declared their conviction
that 'a sole or even a first minister, is an officer
unknown to the law of Britain, inconsistent with
the constitution of this country, and destructive of
liberty in any government whatsoever,' and that
'it plainly appearing to us that Sir Robert Walpole has for many years acted as such . . . we
could not but esteem it to be our indisputable duty
to offer our most humble advice to his Majesty

[1] Todd, *Parliamentary Government in England*, II., p. 152.
[2] *Ibid.*   [3] *Ibid.*, II., pp. 157-158.

for the removal of a minister so dangerous to the king and the kingdom.' " [1] This debate, though not resulting in the dismissal of Walpole, did result in his defeat at the next election, and he resigned largely thus because of the feeling against him as a boss.

After Walpole's loss of office, there was no Prime Minister for several years. As Todd says,[2] "It was not until the accession to office of the younger Pitt in 1783 that the paramount authority of the Prime Minister over his associates in the government was unreservedly confessed; and that as a natural consequence government by departments came to an end." Between Walpole's retirement and the accession to office of William Pitt the younger, it is true that certain ministers were more important and prominent than the others in office at the same time. This was true, for example, of William Pitt the elder, afterward Earl of Chatham. But after Walpole's retirement the government was in the hands of the Whigs, who "displayed little ability for office and much for division and intrigue." [3]

With the accession of William Pitt the younger to office in 1783 the idea of a Prime Minister be-

[1] *Ibid.*, II., p. 158. [2] *Ibid.*, II., p. 151.
[3] Donne, *Correspondence of George III.*, I., p. 37, quoted from Todd, *op. cit.* II., p. 159.

came firmly established. In 1781 the system of government by departments, which was then the acknowledged system, was denounced in Parliament. Lord North referred to it as a very bad system, saying, "There should be one man or a Cabinet to govern the whole and direct every measure."[1] Mr. Todd, in summing up the development of the office of Prime Minister as now understood, says it "has contributed materially to the growth and perfection of parliamentary government. . . . By an easy gradation, the personal authority of the sovereign under prerogative government receded into the background and was replaced by the supremacy of the Prime Minister under parliamentary government."[2]

In other words, the irresponsible leader, the king or his favorite, has given way to the responsible leader or Prime Minister, responsible not merely to Parliament, but as Parliament became responsible to the people, responsible as well through Parliament to the people. "The office of Prime Minister," Mr. Todd adds,[3] "as it is now exercised, is a proof and a result of the necessity which exists in our political system for the concentration of power and responsibility in the hands of one man in whom the sovereign and the nation can alike confide. . . . Nevertheless, strange to say, this of-

[1] Todd, *op. cit.* II., p. 170.   [2] *Ibid.*, pp. 171–172.   [3] *Ibid.*, p. 174.

fice is unknown not only to the law but to the constitution. . . . The Prime Minister is simply a member of the Cabinet who possesses preëminently the confidence of the Crown, and to whom the sovereign has thought fit to intrust the chief direction of the government. But the choice of the Premier, however necessary or notorious, must still be regarded as a matter of private understanding, there being no express appointment of any member of the administration to be Prime Minister."

This short sketch of the development of the English Premier shows, then, that the office originated during one of the most corrupt periods of English political history, that its growth was due in large part to this corruption, and was regarded with the greatest hostility by the English people,— so great, indeed, that the man who more than any other is responsible for it and who has been regarded as one of the most corrupt of English statesmen, so far as concerns the means which he used, indignantly denied that he was a Prime Minister. After his fall the attempt was made to get on without the office, but by the very force of circumstances the English had to acknowledge that Walpole's main idea was right, and set to work not to destroy the boss,— for that is what the Prime Minister is,— but to make him responsible, and having accomplished that purpose now regard the regenerated and responsible boss as an indispensable factor in modern parliamentary government.

But it is to be borne in mind that the original English boss, as seen in the position which Walpole occupied, is quite different from the present English Premier. A comparison of Walpole's methods as derived from the short description already given of them, with the methods employed by the Prime Minister of to-day, brings this out quite clearly. Walpole's methods consisted in intrigue, bribery, and corrupt use of governmental powers, and Walpole's success was due in large measure to his consummate ability in this direction. The present methods of the Prime Minister are more in the nature of deliberation with his colleagues at recognized Cabinet meetings. These are, it is true, secret and unofficial, taking place, indeed, commonly on the occasion of private dinners, and no records are kept of the proceedings. But while unquestionably the personal opinions of many a member of the English Cabinet have been obliged to yield either to the will of the majority or to the policy outlined by the Prime Minister, while in many cases compromises have been made which may have involved the sacrifice of principle on the part of the individual ministers, at the same time the means adopted to bring about harmony in

policy have ceased to have the corrupt character
which, if history is to be believed, attached to the
means employed by Walpole. It is no longer
necessary in order to obtain the desired and necessary harmony to resort to these corrupt means,
because the power of the Prime Minister is recognized. What in the time of Walpole had to be
done by stealth and in an underhand manner, may
now be done in the open and through the exercise
of acknowledged power. This was finally settled
by the celebrated controversy between Lord Palmerston and Lord John Russell on the occasion of
the *coup d'état* of Napoleon III., when Lord Russell read a note in Parliament to the effect that
thereafter it was the wish of the queen that no
despatches be sent by any of her Majesty's ministers which had not been submitted to her Majesty.
Lord Palmerston's disobedience resulted in his
retirement from office. This episode had for its
effect the frank acknowledgment of the power of
the English boss, and really put the seal of legality
and constitutionality upon the institution of the
Prime Minister.

Not only have the methods devised by the first
English boss changed. His position is also greatly
changed. Walpole himself, it is true, was not
absolutely irresponsible. The fact that he was
ultimately driven from power is proof of this.

But he was able by the exercise of very corrupt means to keep himself in office for twenty years, despite a most vehement opposition. He was able, by the purchase in one way or another of members of Parliament, to control that body, and on the occasion of parliamentary elections, through means which, from the moral point of view, were no better, to control the elections. While the parliamentary committee appointed after Walpole's fall did not find evidence of as serious corruption as Walpole had been charged with, it is still true that he was corrupt. One of his most friendly biographers says, " That Walpole was guilty of bribery, that he drew upon the funds of the Treasury to obtain political support, and that he was unscrupulous in his organization of the majority are statements which it is impossible to deny." [1]   The popular belief in his corruption was largely influential in bringing about his fall, for the political atmosphere had already begun to clear.   The Methodist revival is evidence of the changed tone of English life following upon the excesses of the Restoration, and Walpole's methods could not fail to meet reprobation.   As Green says : " Vague, too, and hollow as much of the ' high talk ' of the ' Patriots ' was, it showed that the age of political cynicism, of that unbelief in high sentiments and

[1] Ewald, *Sir Robert Walpole*, p. 455.

noble aspirations which had followed on the crash
of Puritanism, was drawing to an end. Rant
about ministerial corruption would have fallen flat
on the public ear, had not new moral forces, a new
sense of social virtue, a new sense of religion, been
stirring, however blindly, in the minds of English-
men." [1]

Of course, Walpole's downfall was not followed
at once by marked political purity. Indeed, it was
not until after the passage of the Reform Bill of
1832 that modern political ideas began to be generally held. But in the meantime the responsibility of the Cabinet and the Prime Minister had
been pretty well worked out, and the reforms of
1832 made Parliament itself responsible to the
people. Since 1830 the course of English political
development has been marked by the most tremendous advance both in making the entire
administrative system subject to the control of the
Cabinet and Prime Minister wherever the general
interests of the nation are concerned, and in securing the freest possible expression of the public
will.

In the first place the administration has been
highly centralized, as has been pointed out. This
had to be done in order to pull England out of the
slough in which it had been mired through the

[1] *History of the English People*, IV., p. 145.

selfishness of the localities and of the classes which controlled the local governments. This work was begun in the poor law administration, but was later continued in the municipal administration, the sanitary administration, the police administration, the school administration, and the local government system generally.

The result of this movement has been not merely to bring the local administration under the control of the central administration, and in that way under the ultimate control of Parliament, but vastly to increase the efficiency of the entire English administrative system. The number of paupers has been decreased, the death rate has been greatly lowered, municipal government has been successful as perhaps in no other country, the ratio of crime to the population is growing less, which can be said of almost no other country, and the advantages of an education which is both compulsory and free, are being offered to all the children of the land.[1]

The civil service, finally, which for a long time was the refuge of incompetents who possessed political influence and was an important factor in the control of elections, has been reorganized and put on a par with any official system that the

[1] See Maltbie, " English Local Government of To-day." *Columbia University Series*, etc. Vol. IX., No. 1.

world can produce at the present time. It has ceased to be the plaything of politics and has become an efficient instrument of administration.

In the second place, Parliament and the ministers through Parliament have become responsible to the people, who have been in growing numbers admitted to share in the formal expression of the public will through the grant to them of the suffrage. Act after act has been passed to insure the secrecy of the vote and to prevent corrupt practices at elections. The whole tone of English public life has changed.

These are then the changes which have resulted from the frank recognition, that whatever may be the outward form of the government, however popular it may be, the boss or leader is an absolute necessity, and from the determination not to destroy the boss but to make him responsible. As the absolute monarchy seems to the historical student of to-day to have been an unavoidable stage in political development, so must the development of the boss appear to the student of popular government as not only necessary but as salutary. The means to which the absolute monarchy resorted in order to establish and maintain itself were, it is true, often arbitrary and cruel. The means by which the boss develops also seem to be of necessity corrupt and vicious.

What all should remember, however, is that, notwithstanding the boss may be necessary, and notwithstanding the means to which he resorts may perhaps of necessity be corrupt and vicious, it is perfectly possible that the boss that actually develops may not slough off his corruption. It should be borne in mind that for some peoples the absolute monarchy was not merely a stepping stone to better things, it remained a permanent institution. Whether the boss as he is seen at the present day in the United States shall remain as he is or perhaps fall even lower in the scale of political morality, depends largely on the fact whether he remains irresponsible to the people. England's great advance was due not to the fact that she developed a Walpole : it was due to the fact that after she developed a Walpole she saw the defects in her handiwork and proceeded to remedy them until she produced a Pitt, a Palmerston and a Sir Robert Peel.

While therefore the development of the boss in the United States, even when accompanied by the corruption which we are accustomed to ascribe to him, much of which may be exaggerated as in the case of Walpole, is not in and of itself so alarming, we must remember that his irresponsibility as it now exists is a distinct menace to popular institutions, and that his corruption, if allowed to continue,

will destroy the very basis of our political organization. Governments which are both irresponsible
and corrupt have been permanent, and irresponsible government tends to become corrupt government. Popular government in the true sense of
the word cannot long continue to exist if it
becomes irresponsible and corrupt.

On the other hand it may be a source of com-
fort to those who believe in popular government
and in all that it implies, to remember both that
the greatest corruption in England was characteristic of a system of government which in no sense
of the word was really popular, and that this corruption with the system of irresponsible boss government which seemed to thrive upon it was not
done away with in a few years. Walpole himself
was in office for twenty years, and it was not until
more than half a century after he left office that
England's regeneration began. But that regeneration finally came.

Political changes are naturally made more
quickly nowadays, but still it may be years
before our bosses become responsible and cease to
be corrupt. But, in order that they shall be
responsible, and shall cease to be corrupt, it is
necessary for all who want good government to
fight on, now for this reform, now for that one,
always bearing in mind that the ultimate purpose

should not be to destroy the boss as an institution, but to make him amenable to the public will.   In such a fight, it may be necessary to do what can be done to destroy a particular boss, as Walpole was destroyed, but unless history fails to repeat itself, the boss who has fallen by the way will be replaced by another, who, learning wisdom from his predecessor's experience, will approach more nearly the ideal of real popular government, the responsible party leader.

So far, it must be admitted that not much light has been thrown by our consideration of the development of the English Prime Minister upon the problem of making the American boss responsible.   We have, it is true, seen that very soon after the power of the English Crown had been assumed by Parliament, the boss was developed, and that the boss has become responsible to the people through the reform of Parliament and its being made responsible to the people.   This responsibility has been secured in the formal governmental organization, or rather in close connection with the formal governmental organization.   For the English Premier is not even now recognized in any way by law.   But he occupies an official position, and can thus be reached as an officer.   He is, however, not merely an officer, he is a party leader, and his party is in control of the House of

Commons. As soon as he ceases to have the confidence of his party in the House of Commons, or, in case of a parliamentary election, as soon as his party loses the confidence of the people, he ceases to be the boss, and has to step out of office. If his position is analyzed, it will be seen he owes it to the fact that provision is made in the governmental organization for the coördination of the expression and execution of the public will. This being the case, the political storm centre is a governmental organ, that is, Parliament. So far as the parties are concerned, their struggles are directed to getting control of Parliament. That being accomplished, the work of the party is accomplished.

These conditions are not present in the United States. Our formal governmental system makes no provision for the coördination of the functions of expressing and executing the will of the state through the instrumentalities of government. On the contrary, it is so formed as to make that coördination impossible. That is, the work of the party is not completed when it has elected a legislature. It must elect a series of executive officers as well, not only for the nation and the state, but also for the localities. Further, the fact that the terms of these executive and legislative officers are not coincident makes it probable that even if one party has elected all the officers it can elect at a given election, such party does not have complete control of the government. The political storm centre in the United States is therefore not in the government, but in the party. All attempts to make the boss responsible must take account of this fact. The party must be made responsible to the people. After this is done, the boss will have been attacked in his stronghold, and will be forced to capitulate. In that way, and in that way alone, can we hope to see our government conducted by party leaders amenable to popular control.

CHAPTER IX

RESPONSIBILITY OF PARTIES AND PARTY LEADERS

IT has been shown that the American political party is not as responsible to the people as it should be if the governmental system is to be popular in character, and that the American party leader, as a result, is hardly amenable to popular control. It has also been shown that in order that the party leader shall be made amenable the party must become responsible. The question now naturally presents itself, How can this be accomplished? To answer this question we must bear in mind what it is that makes the party irresponsible.

The first cause of the irresponsibility of parties in the United States is to be.found in the work demanded of the party. What that work is, has, it is hoped, been sufficiently dwelt upon. The party in the American political system has to do what in other political systems is devolved upon the formal governmental organization. But the reason that the party does this work is to be found in the character of the governmental system itself.

That is, the party does this work because the governmental system is so formed that it cannot do it, and if the party did not do it we would have anarchy instead of government. Further, the party organization is as strong as it is because the party has to do this work, and as long as the party has to do this work, its organization will probably continue much the same as it is at present.

In other words, if we are to have much change in our party organization, our governmental organization will have to be somewhat changed. Indeed, it has already been shown that our governmental system has changed in the past and is changing at the present time. It has been shown that in nation, state, and municipality the tendency is strongly away from the decentralized administrative system of the middle of the century, and in the direction of administrative centralization.

This change in the governmental organization cannot fail to have its effect on the party, since the party is formed to carry on the government. It will reduce the amount of work demanded of the party, and by so much reduce the necessity for strength in the party organization, which in the past has resulted in giving in the minds of the people great importance to party loyalty and regularity. Indeed, an observer of political parties in the United States cannot fail to notice the greater ease with which voters, of recent years, change their party associations. The independent vote is believed by many to be growing in numbers and influence. This phenomenon is particularly marked in the cities where the change in the direction of administrative centralization has been more marked than elsewhere.

This relaxation of party allegiance is further a perfectly logical result of our recent movement toward administrative centralization. In former times, when more officers were elected than now, a person who split his ballot was in reality almost guilty of political suicide. For in order that there might be coördination between the making of law and the execution of law it was necessary that the same party be in control of the legislative body and all the executive offices. Were this not the case, the executive in its central and local instances might do much to nullify the law. Not only must the legislature and the executive be in accord, but all the various executive officers should be in accord. For the election of one officer by one party, and of another officer by another, might result in a conflict which would quite paralyze the government and make it incapable of action.

Not only does this movement toward administrative centralization tend thus to relax the bonds of party allegiance, it also tends to fix party responsibility. It does this because where the administration is centralized under the direction of one officer, a party is apt at one election to get greater control over the government than it would if the system were decentralized and the terms of different executive officers not coincident. Take, for example, a city election, at which a mayor with large powers of appointment and control over city officers is elected. If a given party elects its mayor it obtains much greater power, for the exercise of which it is recognized to be responsible, than it would obtain if it elected a mayor who had only a small power of appointment, many city officers being elected, and being elected at different times. The party is thus made responsible by the fact that during the particular term for which a mayor with large powers of appointment and control has been elected, the responsibility of the party is incarnated, so to speak, in its choice of mayor. That is, the responsibility is taken out of the party and is placed in the formal governmental organization.

Another change in our governmental system, which might do much to lessen the work of parties, if we may judge from Swiss experience, is the more frequent use of the referendum.

National parties exist in Switzerland, but, their work being comparatively small, owing, among other things, to the complete subordination of the executive to the legislature,[1] their organization is not strong and their machinery is extremely simple.[2] The referendum, which was introduced in 1874, seems to have had the effect of relieving the party of the work of obtaining decisions on important questions of policy. As Mr. Lowell says,[3] " Not only do the different political groups fail to exercise a decisive influence at the referendum, but the institution itself tends in a variety of ways to lessen the importance and increase the stability of parties." This result is due, in his opinion, to the fact that it tends "to split up political issues, and thus prevents the people from passing judgment on the whole policy of a party in power." There is no "necessity of choosing between the programmes of opposing parties and of accepting some one of them in its entirety. The referendum, therefore, deprives political programmes of much of their significance, by allowing the people to elect a representative and then reject any of his measures they do not like."

How far the referendum is applicable to American conditions is, of course, a serious question. American conditions are complex as compared with

[1] *Supra*, p. 89.   [2] Lowell, *op. cit.*, II., p. 313.   [3] *Ibid.*, II., p. 326.

the Swiss.   Wealth is much more evenly distributed in Switzerland than here.   The communities are as a general thing much smaller than here.   The conditions in Switzerland are much more favorable than here for the development of a thoroughly democratic government. At the same time it must be admitted that the attempts we have already made in the direction of the referendum have been followed by considerable advantage, and there is every reason to believe that more frequent resort to it would have a beneficial effect in reducing the amount of work the party has at present to do, and in thus making it more responsive to the public will.

But while much has been done toward diminishing the work of the party, much remains to be done before the governmental system of the United States will be such as to make it easy to secure complete party responsibility.   It is only when the referendum is much more frequently resorted to than at present, and when the entire administrative system is pretty well centralized under an executive, who in his turn is subjected to an effective legislative control, that this result will have been attained.   That such a condition of things will exist in the near future in the United States may well be doubted.   The prospects of securing the immediate and general adoption of the referendum are not bright, while the immediate abandonment of our fundamental principle of the separation of powers and the consequent subjection of the executive to the legislative cannot for a moment be expected.

It is of course true that our national administrative system has been highly centralized, but the relation of the President and Congress is such that lack of harmony, which is impossible of immediate remedy, may at any time arise and is very apt to arise about the middle of each President's term, inasmuch as the House of Representatives is then renewed in its entirety. The term of the Senate is such also as to make it probable that few Presidents will be in harmony during their entire term of office with both houses of Congress.

In our state governments all these opportunities for conflict exist, and in addition thereto most of the important heads of the executive departments of the state government are elected. Not only are they elected, but in many instances they are elected for a term of office not coincident with that of the governor. For they are not in all cases elected at the same time as is the governor, or if so elected do not have the same term as he. Finally, the governor has little power of supervision and control over them. The method of filling these offices, the terms of office, the dates of election, and the relations of the executive and legislature are fixed by the Constitution which, particularly in the case of the national government, is difficult of amendment. The work of the party in our political system must then be for quite a time in the future much the same as it is in the present. No great hope may be entertained that, outside of the cities, the work demanded of it will soon be much diminished.

The irresponsibility of the parties is due, in the second place, to the position which we have assigned to the party. The enormous work which has been devolved upon the American political party, and which it would seem that the party must perform for many years to come, has really made the party a most important political organ. And yet the party is largely a voluntary organization governed by rules of its own making, which are enforced or not, according as their enforcement is or is not to the advantage of the few who have succeeded in getting control of the party machinery. The courts as a general thing refuse to exercise any control over parties.

Their attitude may be seen in an opinion by Judge Hooker given in the case of Stephenson against Boards of Election Commissioners.[1] The

[1] Decided in the Supreme Court of Michigan in the year 1898, and reported in 76 Northwestern Reporter, 915.

judge says, alluding to Michigan party politics:
"From our earliest recollection party politics has
always been a matter of shrewdness and management, not always defensible; yet the people have
been left to deal with the difficulties as they arise.
It is not to be supposed that committees on creden-
tials, however fairly selected, have always dealt
justly; and no doubt expediency or political exi-
gency has governed their actions to the exclusion of abstract justice. The remedy has usually
been either a bolt on the part of the dissatisfied
and the selection of an opposition candidate within
the party, or a refusal by the electors to support
the nominee; and the courts have been careful
not to interfere with the application of these remedies, which have usually been found adequate."

In the case of *In re* Redmond [1] Judge Adams
says: The Election Law "in a variety of ways
recognizes what the experience of all teaches,
—that under our system of government, the
affairs of the state are conducted through the
medium of the representatives of political parties,
and that of necessity such parties must, to a
certain extent, provide for their conduct and
management certain rules and regulations which
are not inaptly termed 'Party Machinery.'
That such machinery is frequently employed to

[1] 25 New York Supplement 38.

accomplish personal and factional ends cannot be denied, that it is sometimes used to crush any expression of sentiment by, and to defeat the desires of, a large majority of the political party it is supposed to represent, is undoubtedly true. But, nevertheless, the party cannot exist without its machinery, and if that machinery is used oppressively and for improper purposes, the right and the power to remedy the evil undoubtedly reside in the party itself." The determination of a party convention "may be unjust; it may be in direct violation of the equities of any given case, and as contended by counsel in theory, it may be right and proper to disregard such an adjudication, and to insist that no party division may exercise any supervisory control over any smaller division. But if such a theory were put into practice, it would be subversive of party discipline and would reduce political parties to mere associations of independent and irresponsible mobs. No such rule as the one contended for, obtains in any voluntary organization, but on the contrary, the very term 'Organization' implies a recognition of order and an obedience to duly constituted authority. These observations lead of necessity to the conclusion that where a person allies himself with a political party, he tacitly acknowledges allegiance to all the rules and regulations of that party as enunciated or expressed by what party usage recognizes as the supreme or superior authority of the organization. The recognition of this principle does not compel one to follow blindly the dictates of party, nor to vote for incompetent or unfit candidates, for he still possesses the inalienable right of severing either permanently or temporarily his party relations; neither does it prevent any person with a sufficient number of followers who desire his election to any office, from being a candidate for that office in the manner provided by the statute. But he cannot claim to be the nominee or representative of a political party unless he has been first regularly nominated by that party; and what constitutes regularity depends, as I think has been shown, upon the usages of the party itself and not upon any rules or regulations which may seem just and proper to courts or judges."

The actual point decided in this case was, that a determination by the state convention of a party on a contest between two delegations as to the regularity of the conventions by which they were nominated, will be treated by the courts as conclusive.[1]

[1] Immediately after the passage of the Australian Ballot Law in New York, which gave the courts power to determine upon the regularity of party nominations, some of the judges, however, showed a tendency to take jurisdiction of these cases, especially where the contest had not been decided by the superior authorities within the

In 1896 the Election Law of New York was amended, so as to provide that if there was a

party. A good case is that of *In re* Woodworth, 16 New York Supplement, 147. In this case on a mandamus to a county clerk to place upon the official ballot the name of one of two contesting candidates the court went into the matter of the regularity of the primary meetings at which the candidates had been nominated, and decided the question. The decision of the court was afterward affirmed by the general term. (64 Hun, 522, also reported in 19 New York Supplement, 525.) Notwithstanding these adjudications, every state convention, every judicial, congressional and senatorial convention of the district in which the case came up, saw fit to ignore the decision, and to recognize the opposing faction as the only lawful representative of the party. Such being the case the question came up again before the Supreme Court at special term, under the name of *In re* Pollard, 25 New York Supplement, 385.

Under these circumstances, the court, the opinion being written by the same judge who made the decision in the first instance, decided that the ruling of the highest authority in the party was to control. The judge remarks that it would " have been no more than courteous for the party convention to have adopted the decision of the general term, which was deliberately made, after a careful and impartial hearing, but there is no way in which they can be compelled to do so, and consequently it seems to me that the only rule for courts and judges to adopt in this and all other similar contests, is that they will interfere only in cases where there has been no adjudication of the question of regularity by some division of the party which is conceded to be superior in point of authority to the one in which the contention arose; provided, of course, that the question of good faith in the making of such adjudication is not involved. The adoption of a different rule will inevitably tend to bring party organizations and the courts into unseemly conflict over questions which are peculiarly within the cognizance of the former tribunals, a result which most certainly ought if possible to be avoided."

division within a party, and two or more factions claimed the same device or name, the secretary of state should decide such conflicting claims, "giving preference of device and name to the convention or primary or committee thereof recognized by the regularly constituted party authority." This section of the Election Law came up before the Court of Appeals.[1] A justice of the Supreme Court had reversed the decision of the secretary of state that one Fairchild was the regular Republican candidate for representative in Congress for the Sixteenth Congressional District. The decision of the Supreme Court was affirmed by the Appellate Division of the Supreme Court, but was reversed by the Court of Appeals. The Court of Appeals, while it admits that its decision was based upon technical reasons relating to the jurisdiction of the judge at special term, still in a dictum, goes into the consideration of the general question. The opinion says: "In this case whether a majority of the delegates in the congressional district favored the nomination of Fairchild depends solely upon the regularity of the election of five delegates elected in the Second Assembly District of Westchester County. In that district an assembly district convention was regularly called. Before its organization, however, a dispute arose between the

[1] In the matter of Fairchild, reported in 151 New York, 359.

delegates, and two separate conventions were organized, each of which elected delegates to the state convention, delegates to the judicial convention and delegates to the congressional convention for the Sixteenth District. When the state convention assembled, the delegates elected by each of these two conventions appeared before the state committee and the state convention, and claimed seats in the latter. The contest arising out of this situation was first brought to a hearing before the state committee, which, after considering the matter, decided that the assembly convention which elected delegates in favor of Fairchild's nomination was the regular and properly organized district convention, and that the delegates elected by it were the duly and properly elected delegates. This contest was then brought to a hearing before the convention, where the matter was again investigated, and the convention reached the same conclusion."

"The effect of the statute, and how far its provisions are binding upon officers in determining these questions, and upon courts or judges in reviewing the determinations of such officers, is a subject upon which the Supreme Court has rendered variant and conflicting decisions — one class holding that the determination of party conventions or party authorities has no weight whatever, while the other class is to the effect that in determining questions as to the regularity of conventions, officers and courts should rely upon the action and determination of the regularly constituted party authorities upon the question where there has been such a determination. We think the latter effectuates the obvious intent and purpose of the statute. . . . We think that in cases where questions of procedure in conventions or the regularity of committees are involved, which are not regulated by law, but by party usages and custom, the officer called upon to determine such a question should follow the decision of the regularly constituted authorities of the party. The courts, in reviewing the determination of such officers, should in no way interfere with such determination. We think an opposite rule would be in conflict with the spirit and intent of the statute, burden the courts with a class of litigation that would be unfortunate and embarrassing, and might produce results entirely at variance with the will of a majority of the electors of the party."

The question, therefore, as to the finality of the determination of the superior or supreme authority in the party as to the regularity of nominations must be considered as settled in New York. What action the courts of New York will take where their action is not prejudiced by the precedent action of the higher party authority is not exactly clear.[1]

The courts of Kentucky agree with the New York Court of Appeals in recognizing the finality and conclusiveness of the determination of the highest authorities in the party. In Cain v. Page,[2] Cain had a majority of some sixty or seventy votes upon the face of the returns of the primary election; but, upon a contest inaugurated by Page before the Democratic county committee, the latter was found to have received the highest

[1] See, also, the case of *In re* Clerk of Clinton County (decided in a special term of the Supreme Court of the state of New York, and reported in 48 New York Supplement, 407). In this case it was held that party usage, not inconsistent with good morals or the letter or spirit of the statute law, is a law to party conventions. The party usage had always been for the chairman of the county committee to call the convention of the party to order. Owing to a trick of the minority, the attention of the regular chairman of the county committee was directed to other matters, and a person belonging to the minority faction of the party called the convention to order, and declared the election of a chairman and clerk who belonged to his faction. The clerk was directed *viva voce* to cast a vote for the delegates of the same faction, and within ten minutes the convention had adjourned. The chairman of the county committee then called the committee to order, and it was held that those who remained in the room constituted the regular convention, and its nominees were given a place upon the party's ticket, to the exclusion of the nominees elected by the other faction.

[2] Decided in the Court of Appeals of Kentucky, in October 1897, and reported in 42 Southwestern Reporter, 336.

number of legal votes, and a certificate of nomination was thereupon issued to him. The action was brought to compel the committee to reassemble, and after cancelling Page's certificate of nomination, to hear and determine any contest that might be brought before it. The basis of the action was that one O'Neal participated in the decision of the contest as a member of the committee, when according to the party law he was not such a member. The action of the committee and of O'Neal had been approved by the supreme authority of the party in the state convention. The court said: "We hold this action of the state convention to be conclusive recognition of the O'Neal committee as the governing authority of the Democratic party in the district in question, beyond which action and recognition the courts cannot go. It is contended for appellees that party usage authorized the selection of O'Neal as chairman of the committee and as a member thereof, although he was not a member of the committee as originally constituted. But the question is an immaterial one in view of the action of the state convention. The voice of that convention was the very voice of the Democratic party. The word of the convention is the law of the party, and the court cannot look beyond this word or this law because there is no other. When counsel questions the authority of the state convention in party organization, it is as if the Mohammedans should doubt the Koran, or the Christian, the Book of Books."

It will be noticed that the decision of the New York Court of Appeals was made in interpreting a statute which practically gave the secretary of state the power to determine which was the regularly constituted authority. In most cases, however, there is no provision of statute on this question. The statute merely provides that any convention of delegates of a political party which presented candidates at the last preceding election may make nominations for public office; and that a convention within the meaning of the act is an organized assemblage of voters or delegates, representing a political party which at the last election before the holding of such convention polled a certain percentage of the votes cast.

Under such statutes it has frequently been the case that there have been contesting rival conventions. The question has thus arisen as to what action the courts will take with regard to placing upon the official ticket the names of the candidates of either convention under the regular party heading.

One of the best cases upon this subject is that of Stephenson *v.* Boards of Election Commissioners.[1] In this case the court decided that the election commissioners had no authority to accept one of the tickets to the exclusion of the other; that both tickets should be printed upon the ballot, and the name of the party as certified should be placed above the tickets without further addition or distinctive designation than such as was contained in the certificate furnished.[2]

A similar case was decided in Colorado,[3] where the court said: " It is his [the secretary of state's] duty to certify both tickets to the county clerk, in order that both may be printed upon the official ballot. By pursuing this course the merits of the opposing candidates will be submitted to the people, the tribunal under our system of government that must ultimately pass upon such questions. The conclusion that the secretary of state should, under the circumstances, certify both sets of nominations to the county clerks to be printed upon the official ballot, is in harmony with the rule of construction which requires the courts, in cases of doubt between two constructions, to follow that which will afford the citizen the greater liberty in casting his ballot."

[1] Reported in the Supreme Court of Michigan, in 76 Northwestern Reporter, 914.

[2] See also Shields *v*. Jacobs, 88 Mich. 164.

[3] See People *v*. District Court, 18 Col. 26 ; 31 Pacific Reporter, 339.

In the case of Phelps *v.* Piper,[1] the court says: "The legislature has not provided any means for determining these controversies. Political parties are voluntary associations for political purposes. They establish their own rules. They are governed by their own usages. Voters may form them, reorganize them, and dissolve them at their will. The voters ultimately must determine every such question. The voters constituting a party are, indeed, the only body who can finally determine between contending factions or contending organizations ; the question is one essentially political and not judicial in its character. It would be alike dangerous to the freedom of elections, the liberty of voters, and to the dignity and respect which should be entertained for judicial tribunals, for the court to undertake in any case to investigate either the government, usages, or doctrines of political parties, and to exclude from the official ballot the names of candidates placed in nomination by an organization which a portion or perhaps a large majority of the voters professing allegiance to the particular party believed to be the representatives of its political doctrines and party government. We doubt even whether the legislature has power to confer upon the courts

[1] 48 Neb. 725; also reported in 67 Northwestern Reporter, at 755.

any such authority. It is certain, however, that the legislature has not undertaken to confer it." [1]

There are, however, a series of cases, mainly in Colorado, which claim for the courts a very large power in reviewing the determinations of the authorities of political parties. Thus in the case of Tapps *v.* Krier,[2] the court held that the votes of delegates to a party convention from a precinct, established by the committee of such party to give the residents thereof representation in its convention, cannot be excluded by the chairman of a political convention.

In the case of Liggett *v.* Bates,[3] the court held, where a convention of a party met in a place provided by the call, and the chairman of the county central committee called it to order, and before the election of a temporary chairman entertained a motion to adjourn to another place, which was declared carried by a *viva voce* vote, and refused to allow a division, that a majority of the convention thereafter remaining and nominating officers constituted the real convention, and said adjournment was unauthorized.

A case involving the same principle was decided

[1] See also the case of State *v.* Johnson, decided in Montana and reported in 46 Pacific Reporter, 440.

[2] Decided in the Supreme Court of Colorado, December, 1898, reported in 55 Pacific Reporter, 166.

[3] Reported in 50 Pacific Reporter, 860.

by the Supreme Court of Nebraska in December, 1898.[1] In this case it was held that a nomination to public office made by four out of twenty-eight members of a county committee chosen by a political party is invalid, where previous notice of the time and the place of the meeting of the committee had not been given to the other members thereof.

The decisions of the courts of the various states thus evidence some conflict on this point, some, like those of the courts of New York and Kentucky, claiming for the decisions of the highest party authority absolute conclusiveness and finality, others in case of contests between party factions refusing to decide between them, and finally, others assuming to exercise a certain degree of control over the actions of party authorities in making nominations, particularly where the decision of the highest party authority has not been had.

It may, however, be said that the actions of party leaders in the management of party affairs are not, under most of the decisions, subject to an effective judicial control. It is left largely to the individual party members by their unaided exertions to bring it about that the affairs of the party are conducted in an honest and fair manner. This can only be done as a result of a prolonged, con-

[1] This is State *v*. Smith, reported in 77 Northwestern Reporter, 584.

tinuous, and bitter struggle, which can ordinarily be conducted with a fair prospect of success only on the condition of the devotion to it of a large part of the time and effort of the contestants. Under such conditions the almost invariable rule is that success will crown the efforts of those alone who are willing to devote practically their entire time to the struggle. These are notoriously those persons who hope to gain some substantial advantage from the struggle. Such persons do not scruple to make use of unfair means in their pursuit of power, largely because such a method of procedure is not effectively prevented by the law.

The unfair means which are most commonly resorted to in order to obtain control of party machinery are of two kinds. The one consists in devices intended to secure an attendance at party meetings favorable to the party leaders. The other is to be found in actual fraud in the count of the vote which is cast at such meetings, if by chance the attendance is not favorable to those in control of the organization. The most common devices by which attendance at nominating meetings favorable to the plans of the party leaders is secured are the holding of party meetings at times and places that are not calculated to bring out a large representation of the parties. Either no general notice of the meeting is given out or the meeting is held in a place which has not been known to the party generally, or is difficult of access.   One of the cases cited would seem to show that in a glaring case of this sort the courts will refuse to recognize such action as proper.[1]

The attempt is also made in one way or another to exclude from voting those whose votes are not desired, and by "repeating" or other such fraudulent practices to swell unduly the number of votes in favor of the party leaders.   Where provision is made for the enrolment of members of the party, such an enrolment is made to include the names of persons, sometimes including the names of those who are deceased, who have really no right to vote or to say anything as to the management of the party, and to exclude those whose votes are not desired, notwithstanding they may be qualified.   Although the rules of the party may provide that such enrolment shall be subject to the scrutiny of all members of the party, it is difficult, if not impossible, in many cases for those who are not in sympathy with the party leaders to get access to it.   Instances are not infrequent where *bona fide* members of the party have been arbitrarily dropped from the rolls or not permitted to vote when their names are inscribed thereon. The enrolment becomes not merely a farce, but

[1] See State *v.* Smith, *supra*, p. 220.

a means as well by which the party leaders continue themselves in power contrary to the wishes of the majority of those accustomed to act with the party at the elections. Where such a condition of affairs has been reached as to deprive the enrolment of all semblance of being representative of the party, the enrolment is "purged" as it is called. But the purging process, being conducted under the supervision of those in control of the party machinery, causes really little change in actual conditions.

There are a few cases, however, where even the courts in New York have held that they will afford relief to voters who have been improperly excluded from the enrolment, or who wish to examine the enrolment. Thus in *In re* Guess,[1] it was held that mandamus will issue to compel a political association to place upon its rolls one who swears that he is an adherent of that party and its principles, that he supported its ticket at the last election and intends to support its principles and candidates in the future. It has also been held by the Appellate Division [2] that where an enrolment of the registered voters in the city,

[1] Decided at a special term of the Supreme Court in 1896, 38 New York Supplement, 91.

[2] See People *ex rel.* Scire *v.* General Committee, 49 New York Supplement, 723.

made for the benefit of the party, is by the party rules open to inspection by any member of that party, the right of a member to inspect, including the right to make a copy of the list of names found there, provided in copying he does not take up unnecessary time or interfere with the right of inspection by any other member, is enforcible by mandamus.

In other cases, no enrolment is provided at all, but the vote at the party meeting is conducted on the principle that all the members of the party are known, and while challenges may be allowed in case some one presents himself whose party membership is not certainly known, such challenge is allowed to be overcome by an oath that the person so presenting himself for the exercise of the right to vote is a *bona fide* member of the party.

Finally, whether provision is or is not made for an enrolment, the determination of the qualifications for party membership is made by the party organization, that is, by the few persons in control of the party, and conditions are generally required which shut out those who have not voted for all the party candidates at the last election. The tendency of the parties is to busy themselves not merely with the elections for national and state officers, for whose election the parties are primarily organized, but also, on account of the close connection between national and local politics, with the election of local officers as well. These conditions often make it necessary, in order that a man may have a theoretical right to act with a party in its nominations of national and state officers, that he shall have voted for the local candidates nominated by the party at the last local elections. Many persons, however, while in sympathy with the national and state politics of a party, may not be in sympathy with its local policy, and *vice versa*, and thus cannot participate at all in the management of the party, and a narrow clique of persons remains year after year in control of the party machinery and take from the party almost altogether its representative character.

The other methods adopted to prevent the voters from participating in the management of the parties, consist in practices of whose fraudulent character there can be no doubt whatever. These are "repeating" in voting, and a false count of the vote. These practices, however reprehensible in theory, are not generally illegal, since the party is a voluntary organization and as such free from effective public control. Those in charge of the party machinery appoint the officers who receive and count the vote and have thus the power, if by any chance the actual vote is against them, so to arrange the published results as may be most satisfactory to them.

It has thus been held in New York that the courts will not review the determination of a county committee of a party that a certain person was elected chairman of a certain election district.[1] In this case an application was made to the court to review by certiorari the decision complained of, and the court held, very largely on account of technical reasons, that a certiorari was not maintainable.

The court says in the course of its decision: " It is not claimed that this political association is acting under statutory authority in determining the validity of elections held under its direction. The Election Law of this state prescribes certain rules and regulations for the holding of primary elections; and the law makes certain corrupt practices at political caucuses and conventions a misdemeanor; but none of the provisions of these statutes constitute the county committee a judicial officer or party authorized by law to hear or determine any question of fact submitted to it, which would be necessary in order to confer jurisdiction on this court to review their determination in this proceeding. The county committee has acted

[1] See People *ex rel.* Trayer *v.* Lauterbach, 7 Appellate Division Reports, 293.

upon evidence satisfactory to itself that the relator was not elected chairman of this association. Article 8 of the constitution of the county committee provides that all contests as to the election of election district officers or members of the campaign committees shall be investigated by the committee on appeals, and shall be decided by the county committee. This election in question was duly investigated by the committee on appeals and was decided by the county committee, and in this proceeding we have no power to review that determination."

If, as the result of extraordinary vigilance and activity, the opponents of those in control of the party succeed in preventing those not qualified to vote from voting, and actually secure an honest count, so that the result is in their favor, their action is not infrequently nullified by the device of a contesting delegation whose claims are upheld in the convention to which the delegation goes. This is done through the power the party leaders have in the higher instances of party control. In fact all appeals from the decisions of party managers go merely to higher authorities in the party, and are generally decided in favor of the party management. These decisions it has been shown are not generally subject to judicial review.

The following is a sample of the things which

persons have to contend with, who, while believing in party government and desiring to participate in the management of the party, are dissatisfied with the party machine. It is taken from an address made to the members of one of the national parties in one of the large cities in the United States. It reads : "The party machine has forfeited . . . confidence . . . also because of the notorious facts that its enrolment is largely fictitious, that every attempt to purge the rolls is resisted, and appeals are in most instances overruled and in many cases not even heard; that inspection of the rolls is uniformly denied, except to those in accord with the leaders, and is denied even to candidates for party nominations who are opposed by the leaders. Delegates to conventions are prevented from inspecting the preliminary rolls to be used in the organization of those conventions, as well as the enrolments of the various election districts upon which the election of delegates is claimed to be based. Committees appointed by the machine to pass upon the qualifications of delegates at such conventions overrule protests and refuse to investigate charges of fraudulent enrolments and elections. Such abuses of administration and such methods of control exist within the machine that representative government and the rule of the majority have virtually disappeared. The machinery of organization is perverted to defeat honest representation and is used to carry out the will of a small minority."

Continued failure in the attempt to oust objectionable party managers has its natural result in the abstention of the most valuable elements of the party from participation in party management. In some cases the indignation of this element is so strong that they may attempt to rebuke the party management by voting at the elections for the candidates of the opposite party. Such a proceeding, however, generally results merely in putting the other party in power and as both of the leading parties are managed in accordance with the same ideas, nothing is accomplished in the direction of making the party leaders amenable to the party will.

These are, then, the main evils by which the present party system in the United States is accompanied. They relate, first, to the ascertainment of the persons who may vote in the party meetings, and second, to the methods by which the vote once cast shall be counted. They are evils which arise from the fact that the party, being recognized as a voluntary association, is not subject to effective regulation and control. They are evils, further, which, when presented as they were at one time at the public elections, were cured by extending more and more the control of the gov-

ernment over the elections. Repeating and colonization, ballot-box stuffing, and false counting
were once characteristic of the elections in almost
all the states of the union. In those which have
passed the most stringent laws relative to registration, watching at the polls, and inspection of
the vote, these evils are almost a thing of the past.
At one time bribery and intimidation of voters
were very common. The Australian Ballot Act,
while it has not caused them to disappear, has
greatly reduced the frequency of their occurrence,
and it is believed, if properly amended so as to
make the ballot absolutely secret, would prevent
their occurrence almost completely.

The question naturally arises, Would a treatment of primary elections similar to that which
has been accorded to public elections have the
same result? First, let us take up the question of
the registration of the party members. The need
of some provision of this sort has been felt in the
parties themselves, and the attempt is often made
in the various party constitutions and by-laws to
insist upon a registration of some sort. The
attempts so far made in this direction, however,
have been ineffective, largely, it is believed, because
there is no way possible of enforcing the observance of the rules adopted so long as the enrolment or registration is in the hands of purely

voluntary organizations which are not subject to the pains and penalties of the law — in other words, are not subject to public control. In other cases it has been attempted to give to the rules and regulations of the party organizations the sanction of law by providing that their non-observance shall be punishable. These attempts have also been ineffective, largely because of the natural reluctance of courts and juries to punish as a crime the non-observance of regulations made, not by the public, but by private organizations. Further, such regulations can never be satisfactory because, being made and enforced by private organizations, they naturally cannot offer the same guarantee of impartiality as would regulations made by governmental authority.

Convinced of the ineffectiveness of such provisions, some states, of which Kentucky and New York may be cited as examples, have taken a long step in the direction of the legal recognition of parties as political bodies, by providing in the law for the registration of party voters.[1] This is done by giving the citizen the right, generally at the time he registers for the purpose of voting, of stating the party to which he belongs. The names of those thus stating their party affiliations, with the names of those who specially register, in the

[1] Dallinger, *op. cit.* 185, New York Primary Law of 1898.

way provided by law, subsequent to the official registration, constitute the registers or enrolment lists of the parties for the purposes of their primaries.

Similar in principle to the Kentucky method is the method provided in some other states, of which California is an example. By this method the primary election officers, who are recognized as public officers, must receive the vote of any person who makes oath that it is his *bona fide* present intention to support the nominees of the party with which he is then acting and voting. It has been said that this method is similar in principle to that adopted by the Kentucky law. By this it is meant that both adopt frankly the principle that the party is not a private but a public organization, to which each citizen, as a result of his citizenship, has a right to belong, regardless of his political conduct in the past. This right is, in either plan, limited by the fact that no one can belong to more than one party at a given time. Its exercise is finally assured to him by the protection which the state throws about him, by forcing the party to recognize it.

Some such solution of this question would seem to be inevitable if the party is to be recognized to be what it really is, *i.e.* a political organ. For if the party is a political organ, membership in it and the right to participate in its actions should be protected by the same safeguards which are thrown about the citizen's right to register for the purposes of public elections. If they are not, his right to vote at public elections is deprived of half of its value. It really consists only in the right to choose between two or three candidates in whose nomination he has had nothing to say. What the voter should have, if his right to vote is to be of real importance, is to say not merely that he prefers one of two or three candidates, but that he does not wish any of those proposed. This he naturally cannot have if he is allowed to vote merely at public elections. This he can have if he is guaranteed the right to vote at nominations as well as at elections. The right to nominate he cannot have so long as any body of private persons can refuse to recognize his party membership.

Such a method of party registration, that is, of determining party membership, will not naturally commend itself to those who still entertain the belief that the party is a private and not a political organization. With such persons, argument in its favor is useless. It is hoped, however, that enough has been already said, perhaps not to convince such persons, but at any rate to set them to thinking about the vast amount of work which our political system devolves upon the political party, and it may be to instil doubts into their minds as to whether, when the actual position of the political party in our system is considered, the attitude they hold is correct.   There are others who, while perhaps not disposed to insist on the private and voluntary character of parties, are still of the opinion that this method of determining party membership is open to abuse, in that it permits persons not *bona fide* members of the party, to exercise a control over its actions.   Such an objection is, it must be admitted, not devoid of force.   It is still to be remembered, however, that it is based largely on the theory that party membership is to be determined by past action rather than by present intention.   This theory, if adopted, seriously limits the rights of the citizen, inasmuch as it presupposes that no one as a result of his citizenship has the right to do more than exercise a choice at the polls between candidates, all of whom are objectionable, and in the selection of none of whom he has had anything to say.   The voter's choice is not in reality free if he is precluded in any way from participation in the selection of candidates.

The objection that such a method permits the members of one party to dictate the nominations of another, which is often made, not only rests upon the false idea of party membership which has just been referred to, but can be made to any system of purely private enrolment which can be devised. It not only can theoretically be made to any such system, but, as a matter of fact, it is susceptible of easy proof that party leaders have in the past made use of the voters of other parties to secure control of their own party. Finally, if present intention, and not past action, is made, as it should be, the ground of party membership, this objection falls to the ground as far as theory is concerned. For it is usually provided under such a system as has been outlined, that no one can participate in more than one primary. This being the case, the primary of one party consists only of its own members. So far as practice is concerned, it has not been objectionable in the least. There is usually sufficient rivalry among the party leaders of each party to make it necessary for them to use all their voting strength in their own party. This rivalry makes it impossible for them permanently to exercise any appreciable influence over nominations other than those in their own party. It may of course happen that occasionally such an attempt may be made, but even admitting that this may be the case, the condition of things is not as bad as it is under a system of private enrolment, which permits persons to vote at the primary elections of both important parties, and under which, in most of our large cities, the decisions of one party have been more than once influenced by the aid which its leaders have derived from the members of the other party.

Such a method of determining party membership has, further, the great advantage of permitting a clearer distinction in the national and state parties of local and municipal from state and national issues.   A national party by adopting specific municipal issues may attract to it as party members many persons who, while in sympathy with its municipal policy, would not act with it if not permitted to share in the work of nomination. By permitting them to determine their party membership themselves in a local campaign, they will give the party with whose municipal policy they are in sympathy, their aid, regardless of their or its attitude on national or state questions.   Municipal parties, which, whatever advantages are claimed for them, certainly tend to break up the national parties, considered apart from their municipal policies, would be unnecessary.

Our conclusion is that there is no theoretical or practical objection to making party registration a public matter nor to providing that it shall take place in much the same manner and surrounded with much the same safeguards as the registration of voters for public political elections, and that such a method, if properly applied, has the great advantage of allowing municipal interests to be considered apart from national and state issues.

Can now the principles which have been applied to voting at public elections be in the same way applied to voting at primary elections? If a method of primary voting similar to the one now adopted at public elections is provided, the voting may take place at the same time and place as the registration of voters, for the purpose of public elections and subject to the control of the same officers who have control of such registration. If this is the case, the application to primary voting of the principles applicable to public elections will not involve much increase in the expense of the conduct of elections, which is, since the adoption of the Australian ballot, already considerable. Such a method of primary elections is proposed by the Republican League of Buffalo, New York, after a thorough investigation of primary legislation and plans for primary reform. It is proposed that in each election district on the first day of registration, all citizens at the time of registration shall, after replying (such a reply not being obligatory) to the question with which party they desire to affiliate, be permitted to vote on ballots furnished by the officers in charge of the registration for the persons whom they desire to represent the party. These persons may be nominated either as delegates to party conventions, if such conventions are held, or if the nomination is made directly by the party voters, as the candidates of the party at the coming election.

It is claimed for this plan that one act on the part of the voter suffices for registration for voting at regular elections, for party enrolment, and for primary voting; that the time and place for the performance of the acts necessary for the participation of the party member in the action of his party are made as public as are the time and place of registration, which are notorious and will hardly escape the notice even of those who are not active in the performance of their party duties; and that provision is made for governmental control of registration and of voting at primary elections without unduly increasing the expenses of the government.

This plan permits of the retention of the present convention system, or of the adoption of the system of direct voting for candidates, which is preferred by many. Even if it is felt that the convention system cannot in all cases be abandoned, provision can be made in this method of primary voting for instruction of delegates. Such provision for the instruction of delegates is made under the present Massachusetts law, which allows to be printed on the ballot given to the voter at the primary election (which, though subject to governmental regulation, is not in Massachusetts held on the day of registration) a statement indicating for what principles and which candidate the delegate will vote at the convention to which he may be elected. Under the recent California law, the objection of extra expense is obviated by providing for the compulsory, unpaid service of primary election inspectors, who are to be appointed by the board of election commissioners.

It would seem that if primary voting is made to take place for all parties on the same day and at the same place as the registration of voters, all the operations necessary on the part of the party voter for putting the regular party candidates in the field can be done under public regulation without any material increase in election expenses, and without in any way increasing the burden imposed on the voter. Such a solution of the question actually lessens the burden of the voter, who in addition to voting at elections must, under present conditions, take part as well in the primary. Such a method presupposes personal registration and that the first day of registration shall antedate considerably the day of election. It is difficult to see any serious objection to such a change, except that if the convention system of nominating the candidates for state offices is adopted, the state election campaign will of necessity be made a very short one. Perhaps on this account it would be advisable to try the plan first in the larger cities, and to make it applicable therein only to nominations for local officers and for members of the legislature, whose election campaigns are even now not of long duration. If the convention system is abandoned and nomination by direct vote at such a public primary, as it may be called, is adopted, no such objection is valid.

While nomination by direct vote without the intervention of the convention would seem to be the logical result of the application of the principles of democracy, it is still a method to which serious objections may be advanced. Under such a system the decision by a plurality would seem to be necessary. Decision by plurality would, however, in the majority of cases probably result as does the plurality principle in the public elections where more than two candidates are in the field, in a decision by the minority. The larger the district for which the candidate would be chosen, the greater would be such danger, while in a district so large as the state itself it is possible that such a system could not be made to work at all satisfactorily. Certainly until a large majority of the states adopted such a system of primary elections, it would be necessary to make some special provision for the nomination of delegates to the national convention.

It is probable, further, that if the attempt were made to adopt the principle of direct voting for candidates, conventions would be held for the selection of candidates for the primary elections, as they are now held for the selection of party candidates for the public elections. The net result of the adoption of the direct vote would be thus the addition of another election to our present electoral system. This election would take place, however, on the days of registration. It would not, therefore, add materially to the burden of the voter and would probably have the effect of making the party more responsible to the people. This result would further be accomplished without direct interference with the details of the internal management of party organizations. The decisions which have already been referred to at length,[1] show how reluctant the courts are to interfere. All that the first vote as outlined above would do, would be to make the party organization submit its chosen candidates to the suffrage of the voters of the party before it could declare that they were the choice of the party, and, as the choice of the party, be entitled to places on the official ballot.

Finally the same reasons that have led to the adoption of the Australian ballot would make it necessary probably to adopt for primary elections,

[1] *Supra*, p. 206.

the principles at the bottom of that method of voting. In the nature of things, the form of ballot which would have to be adopted would be the blanket ballot, with the names of the candidates alphabetically arranged under a heading indicative of the office for which the candidates desire to run. For party factions would probably never assume the importance in the relations of the parties which the parties have assumed in the relations of the political system as a whole, and to whose importance has been due the adoption of the party column ballot at such elections.

If some such system as the one outlined is adopted, the party will have received full and frank recognition as a political organ of government of great importance. This recognition will have been accompanied by its subjection to public regulation, and by the guarantee to the individual citizen of the right, in virtue of his citizenship, to participate in the actions of the party. But this frank recognition of the real position of the party in the political system will make necessary a careful definition of the party in the law so regulating it. This has been done heretofore very generally in the Australian ballot acts, and the method there adopted may be followed in the laws regulating the primary elections. This consists in declaring a party to be any organization putting candidates in the field which at the last election polled a certain percentage of the vote. In some cases, as, for example, in Illinois, the law declares that no party thus defined can have the names of its candidates printed on the official ballot at the election unless these candidates have been nominated in accordance with the provisions of the Primary Elections Law.

So long, however, as parties are thus defined, some provision must be made, as has been pointed out, for nomination by persons not belonging to a political party. For the citizen as a result of his citizenship ought to have the right not merely to act with an existing political party, he ought also to be empowered to act outside of the party in the nomination of candidates. For this reason he should have the right, under reasonable restrictions, to join with others of like mind with him in a petition or nomination paper.

The reasons which make it thus necessary to permit a citizen, irrespective of his party affiliations to join in the making of nominations outside of party lines apply with even greater force to granting him as a party member the right to propose persons whose names shall be put on the ballot at the primary elections. The Kentucky law goes furthest of any in according him this right, providing that the name of any person who presents himself in the proper way must be put on the ballot of the party. Massachusetts does not accord such liberal privileges, providing that any five voters can thus make a nomination to be voted on at a primary election. Such a method of proposing candidates for nomination by the party, it may be said, would weaken the party organization. It is, however, questionable whether in the end it would. This method merely takes from the "organization" the monopoly of nomination it now possesses, and subjects it to competition. It would seem to be probable also that any party which really adopted such a method of nomination would have greater chance of success at the polls than a party which clung to the present methods. For its nominees would unquestionably have a more cordial support from the members of the party generally.

The present Primary Elections Law of New York,[1] which is both one of the latest and one of the most radical on the subject, is based upon this desire to give parties legal recognition and to subject their action to judicial control. It provides, in the first place, for the enrolment of party members, giving all persons who have not participated in the primary of any other party during the year the right to enroll in any of the parties.

[1] L. 1899, chap. 473.

There is a distinction made between state parties for which this law has been passed, and local parties; participation in a local party not precluding the participant from participation in a state party. The act further provides for the holding of primary elections under official control, making it necessary that full notice of these elections shall be given, and that they shall be held in proper places, that is, in rooms not more than one story from the street, and not in any way connected with liquor saloons. The primary elections which may be held under the act may be held either for delegates for conventions or, in case the party shall adopt the method, for the direct nomination by the party members of candidates for public office. The officers acting at public elections shall act also at the primary elections, and the oath which they are required to take by the Election Law shall include their duties as primary election officers, and all duties prescribed by the Primary Election Law. The election is by secret ballot. The ballots are not, however, furnished by the state. Provision is made for the presence of watchers, not exceeding one for each district, who may be appointed by any political committee, or by any two or more of the persons whose names are upon the tickets to be voted for at the primary election. The canvass of the votes is conducted in the same way as is the canvass of the votes after public elections. Further, the action of all party officers or members of a political convention, or any inspector of election, or of any public officer or board, with regard to the right of any person guaranteed by the act, or any duties prescribed for any authority by the act, is reviewable by the appropriate remedy of mandamus or certiorari, as the case may require. The courts are also given summary jurisdiction upon complaint of any citizen to review such action or neglect. And in reviewing such action or neglect the court or judge shall consider, but need not be controlled by, any action or determination of the regularly constituted party authorities upon the questions arising in reference thereto, and shall make such decision and order as under all the facts and circumstances of the case justice may require. Finally, the courts may, upon application, issue a subpœna to any elector applying therefor, requiring any person within the same county or city in which a convention is about to be held, to appear before such convention and testify before a committee on contested seats, and to produce public records, or records of a primary election, or a convention of the party of which such convention is about to be held. And any person who desires to contest the right of any other elected to a seat in a convention shall file a notice of such contest, which shall be transmitted to the person whose seat is to be contested. No convention composed of delegates elected in accordance with the acts, shall be held until after the primary day upon which delegates thereto, or delegates to a convention to elect delegates thereto, shall have been elected.

Such are some of the methods which have been proposed or adopted in order to subject the party to public regulation and control as a political organ. In brief, they consist in making the determination of party membership largely, if not entirely, a matter of individual choice, and in causing the counting of the votes at these primary elections for either delegates, where the convention system is adopted, or for candidates, where the direct vote is adopted, to be done by officers, in some cases really public officers, in other cases acting under public control. If a proper method is adopted, the work of the voter who desires to participate with his party in the nomination of candidates may be much lessened, inasmuch as registration, party enrolment and primary voting will occur at the same time and place and under police control. This time and place will further be notorious, a matter of common knowledge.

That such a method, however, will result in the abolition of what has been called the "parlor caucus," and that nominations will be the result of direct, positive deliberation on the part of the members of the party generally, is not for a moment to be anticipated. In case the convention system is adopted, it may be expected that the party leaders will make their "slates" as heretofore, and in case the direct vote is adopted, party conventions prior to the primary election will probably be called together in the future. But it will be possible for the party members to break "slates" more easily under such a system than under the present one, and such conventions will probably be more under their control, particularly if the law makes provision for the instruction of delegates. In the case of the direct vote, party candidates would probably in many instances be the choice of a minority of the party members, but that minority would be larger than is the minority which at present selects party candidates, and by so much would the responsibility of the party leader to the party be increased.

It may be said that this is not much of a gain over the present methods of party nomination. It is to be remembered, however, that if the characterization of democracy which has been made is a true one, — that is, if the attainable in democratic government is not so much the deliberate choice of officers and the positive determination of policies by the people, as the power of veto and the power to change party leaders, — this method of primary elections will do much to make the party, and through it the boss, responsible. For it will put into the hands of the people the same control over nominations as they now have over elections. The people will not be confined in their political action to choosing between two undesirable candidates. They will also have the power to prevent the running, as candidates of their party, of persons in whom they do not have confidence. The same is true also of the general policy of the party. At present formulated in its outward expression by conventions over whose deliberations the average party member has little, if anything, to say, if this method of primary elections is adopted such policy will be determined by bodies much more than at present representative of the party membership.

Nor must the expectation be entertained that any method of primary elections or the complete recognition of the public character of the political parties will result in the disappearance of the boss. Party leaders will always be necessary. The development of responsible party government in England has been, as has been pointed out, accompanied by the recognition of the party leader whose influence should largely dominate the policy of the party, and to whom other party leaders were largely subordinated. Indeed, the recognition of such a party leader seems to have been necessary to the development of responsible party government. Such a leader is, however, responsible to the party, which can force him at any time to step down and out and to give place to one more in harmony with the wishes of the party.

The English party leader, or boss, however, occupies a responsible position in the government as well as in the party, and the fact that he is responsible to the party is largely dependent upon the fact that he has a responsible position in the government. Whether a successful attempt to make the boss responsible to the party is dependent on his assuming a responsible place in the government, no one can say. If it is, all attempts at party reorganization which have for their end the making the boss responsible are, of course, foredoomed to failure. It is believed, however, that the difference between the English and the American system of government, which consists largely in the fact that the party in the United States has to do outside of the government much that is in England done in the government, makes it probable that a party boss may be made responsible to the people by making him responsible to the party, although he may not occupy any important governmental position. The universal demand now being made in the United States for a change in the primary laws would seem to indicate that the people of the United States are generally of the belief that the next step in our political development is to recognize that the party is really a political organ, and should therefore be subjected to public control in the hope of securing responsible popular government— a kind of government which the people are beginning to think they have already lost or are on the point of losing.

No discussion of this question may be regarded as complete without some reference at least to the relations of corporations to parties and party leaders. The enormous development of corporations within the past fifty years has had an influence on our methods of political action. The more recent movement toward the consolidation of smaller corporations into greater corporations — trusts as they are generally though incorrectly called — has likewise had its effect. The relations of these bodies to the government are dependent on one of two things, and generally on both.

In the first place, these corporations are engaged in business whose extent and profit are dependent on positively favorable governmental action.

Some wish a tariff bill adopted which will diminish if not destroy foreign competition. Others desire the grant of public franchises.

In the second place, the development of corporations has resulted in the development of new subjects of taxation. Our original tax laws have almost universally failed in reaching corporate securities in the hands of the individual holders. The continual increase of the expenses of government, due to the increase in the extent of governmental activity, has made it necessary to seek new sources of income. The demand is therefore made that corporations and the new subjects of taxation due to their development shall bear their share of the public burden.

We have thus on the one hand the government with favors to grant and with burdens to impose. We have on the other hand the corporations anxious for favors and desirous to escape burdens. We have also on the one hand a governmental and party system of such a character as not to insure full responsibility for political action. We have on the other hand corporations whose affairs are not as yet conducted with as great publicity as might be desired. In other words, we have conditions which, from the points of view of both temptation and opportunity, favor the establishment of improper relations between those in control of the political system and those in control of our greatest financial, industrial, and commercial institutions. The financial resources of these institutions may, because of this lack of publicity, without serious danger of discovery be placed, however illegally, at the disposal of those in charge of our political institutions. Those in charge of our political institutions may in their turn, because of the irresponsible character of our political system, grant favors to and fail to impose or impose just or unjust burdens on the corporations without serious danger of being held by the people to account for their actions.

It is commonly believed that such improper relations do, as a matter of fact, exist between some of our present large corporations and some of our political leaders. Whatever may be the foundation for this belief, it cannot be denied that the conditions which have been described, do favor the establishment of such relations. If these suspected relations do actually exist, it cannot be denied either that they are in some if not in large measure answerable for the irresponsibility of our political leaders. Any proposals for diminishing this irresponsibility must take them into account.

What now can be done to make such relations impossible, or at least less easy of establishment?

The only answer is publicity. Corporation accounts should be made more public. Accounts of political parties should be made more public. To England again we may look for help. Her corrupt practices acts, which attempt to confine the disbursement of moneys in election campaigns to a single person, who is held to strict accountability, have done much to do away with the illegitimate use of money at public elections. We should probably have to take the further step of prohibiting contributions by any person for purposes of election or nomination to any one except the authorized representative of a political party, who in his turn should be obliged to account for all he had received and spent. A bill of this sort has been introduced recently into the legislature of the state of New York, but as yet has failed of passage.

Proper primary legislation and proper regulation of the relations of corporations and party leaders with the object of securing complete publicity, would seem to be necessary in the United States if we are to hope to make our party leaders and our parties responsible in the management of our government.

CHAPTER X

CONCLUSIONS

THE attempt has been made to show that the securing of popular government and efficient administration, which should be the chief ends of all political systems, may be furthered in the United States by a reasonable concentration and centralization of our present administrative system and by the legal recognition of the political party as a governmental organ. It is not to be expected, however, that mere changes in the administrative system, unaccompanied by this recognition of the party, will of themselves tend to secure either responsible popular government or efficient administration: any more than will the mere recognition of the party as a governmental organ.

Centralized administration without responsible parties will not insure efficient administration, since it lends itself to political manipulation almost as readily as a decentralized system of local self-government, such as we have had in the United States. Under it, it is almost as difficult as under a system of local self-government to separate administration from politics. Centralized administration accompanied by decentralized and weakly organized parties leads in a popular government — that is, a government in which the people have the ultimate control of the execution as well as the making of law — to much the same result as decentralized administration and centralized and strongly organized parties.

Centralized administration combined with a weak party system, while making provision for the responsible leader in its governmental organization, prevents his development in the party by the form which it gives to its party organization. Decentralized administration combined with a strong and irresponsible party system, while making no provision for a responsible leader in its governmental organization, sees an irresponsible boss develop in its party organization. The absence of the party leader in the French and Italian systems results, notwithstanding the existence of a centralized administrative system, in an inharmonious, corrupt, and fitful management of government which sometimes borders on actual anarchy. The presence of the irresponsible boss in the United States political system tends to produce a management of public affairs which is irresponsible, which is often corrupt and extravagant, and is, on account of its irresponsibility rapidly making the maintenance of a continuous policy on the part of the people almost impossible. This is true because the people in their disgust at finding their bosses less responsive to their wishes than they desire, blindly throw off one boss, only to find themselves in control of another of the same sort.

The recognition of the party as a political organ without the reduction of the work assigned to it under the present political system of the United States, would not of itself seem to insure entire popular government or efficient administration. For the work of coördinating the two functions of expressing and executing the will of the state, is so great that it cannot be performed unless the party has great strength. The party leader, whose existence is necessary, must have large powers. Taking advantage of the fears of the people that anarchy or incapacity for progress will result from their too strict demand for observance of their views, he easily degenerates into the irresponsible boss. A decentralized system of government, on account of its very unconcentrated character, makes it difficult to fix responsibility for political action. The control over parties which will result from the recognition of their public position will be exercised by governmental organs. The responsibility for its exercise will, therefore, like that for the discharge of any other governmental function, be difficult to place.

The legal recognition of the party will not result in and of itself in efficient administration, since the decentralized character of the administrative system tends to cause all offices to be regarded as political in character.   Administrative decentralization of itself promotes party irresponsibility, in that it encourages the use of illegitimate means to perpetuate and strengthen the party.

If, then, we hope in the United States to secure popular government and efficient administration, a reasonably centralized administrative system is necessary.   Such a system lessens the work of the party, in that it devolves it upon the government. It tends therefore to make the government more responsible.   For it makes provision for doing in the open, and thus subject to public control, what under a decentralized system is done in secret and not subject to public control.   It tends also to secure efficient administration, in that it makes it possible to relieve a host of officers from political control.

Not only must our system of government be subjected to a reasonable degree of centralization from the administrative point of view, but the party must receive pretty full legal recognition. Such recognition does not involve the destruction of strong national parties nor that of party leaders. Indeed, such destruction, or the substitution of weak local parties for the national parties, would seem highly inexpedient if we are to judge by French and Italian conditions. But the present boss ought to be made responsible to the party and the party responsive to the popular will. The people, if the government is to be popular, should have the power to veto propositions made by party leaders, to deprive them of their leadership, and to intrust the conduct of affairs to others more in accord with the popular will.

Both these results have been secured in the past by recognizing the party, not as a necessary evil, but as the basis on which popular government rests, and by recognizing the boss or party leader — call him what you will — as necessary to the existence of the party. In England this has been done in the governmental system. In this country the same methods may not be applicable. It may, however, be possible to obtain the same results outside of the formal governmental system. But to obtain these results the party must be made responsible. To make the party responsible, it must, so far as its power of nomination is concerned, be recognized as a political organ and subject to public control.

The people of the United States have already

begun to see the need of a change in their administrative system. They have already begun to centralize the administration in the nation, the state, and the city. They are also fast recognizing that there is a function of government which, like the judicial function, should be free from the influences of politics. This is seen in the demand which is being universally made, that the schools and certain city departments, such as the police and fire departments, shall be "taken out of politics," as the current phrase runs. It is also seen in the civil service reform movement, which seems to grow in strength as the years roll by. The people have only just begun to pay attention to the other side of the problem, that is, making the party and party leaders responsible to the people. But they are now demanding with increasing emphasis that the party shall no longer be considered a voluntary organization, but a political body, so far as concerns its power to nominate candidates for public office, and must be subject to public regulation and control.

What those interested in the improvement of our present political conditions should do, then, is not to decry party and attempt to destroy the party leader, nor to oppose all attempts at administrative centralization, as indicative of our degeneration from the faith of our ancestors; but, frankly recognizing that new conditions need new measures, do what can be done in a practical, common-sense way, to secure both responsible government and administrative efficiency. We have too long been shouting battle-cries suitable only to an age that has already passed away. We have been too prone to marshal our forces against tendencies too strong to be resisted, because they are based on verities, — verities, indeed, which we have not as yet comprehended. We should abandon our tilt against windmills, and attack our real foes before they become so intrenched in power as successfully to resist all assault. For it is possible that the irresponsible boss system, which is now developing, may become so firmly established as to make its overthrow extremely difficult, if not impossible. Popular government has been lost in the past, even while its outward forms have been preserved. There is no reason to suppose that it may not be lost again.

On the other hand, we should always remember that the development of the corrupt boss in England in the eighteenth century was made use of by our kin across the sea, as a means for the establishment of as responsible popular government as the world has yet seen. Out of the grave of Walpole arose the English Prime Minister of the present, so sensitive to public opinion that the work of a day almost may cause his overthrow. We should also remember that out of the corruption and inefficiency of the English administrative system of the early part of this century, which made the old English poor law administration a solemn warning, both to economists and administrators, and the English municipal government of the time a byword and reproach, have arisen an administrative system hardly excelled by any other, so far as its efficiency and honesty are concerned, and a system of municipal government which is held up to us as a model for our imitation.

Finally, we should remember that the aristocratic conditions of England cannot be held responsible for the present enviable conditions of English government, any more than the evils from which we suffer are due to democracy. For England was most aristocratic when she was most corrupt. Her great reforms date from the passage of the Reform Bill of 1832, when she began to take on a more democratic character, a character which, it may be added, has, since 1832, been continually increasing in its democracy. Her success in obtaining, on the one hand, popular government, and on the other, efficient administration, has been due in large part to the application of Anglo-Saxon common sense to her political problems, — a common sense which, it is believed, we share with her;

a common sense, further, which refuses to be influenced by the dictates of any fixed political theories, but is willing to use any practicable means at hand, regardless of their consistency with what may have been believed to be the theory at the bottom of the government.   Let us follow her example, not so much in attempting any exact imitation of what she has done, as in adopting her frame of mind and in evincing the same willingness which she has shown, to adapt her governmental system to changed conditions.

INDEX